Perspectives on
Business Intelligence

Synthesis Lectures on Data Management

Editor
M. Tamer Özsu, *University of Waterloo*

Synthesis Lectures on Data Management is edited by Tamer Özsu of the University of Waterloo. The series will publish 50- to 125 page publications on topics pertaining to data management. The scope will largely follow the purview of premier information and computer science conferences, such as ACM SIGMOD, VLDB, ICDE, PODS, ICDT, and ACM KDD. Potential topics include, but not are limited to: query languages, database system architectures, transaction management, data warehousing, XML and databases, data stream systems, wide scale data distribution, multimedia data management, data mining, and related subjects.

Perspectives on Business Intelligence
Raymond T. Ng, Patricia C. Arocena, Denilson Barbosa, Giuseppe Carenini, Luiz Gomes, Jr., Stephan Jou, Rock Anthony Leung, Evangelos Milios, Renée J. Miller, John Mylopoulos, Rachel A. Pottinger, Frank Tompa, and Eric Yu
2013

Semantics Empowered Web 3.0: Managing Enterprise, Social, Sensor, and Cloud-based Data and Services for Advanced Applications
Amit Sheth and Krishnaprasad Thirunarayan
2012

Data Management in the Cloud: Challenges and Opportunities
Divyakant Agrawal, Sudipto Das, and Amr El Abbadi
2012

Query Processing over Uncertain Databases
Lei Chen and Xiang Lian
2012

Foundations of Data Quality Management
Wenfei Fan and Floris Geerts
2012

Incomplete Data and Data Dependencies in Relational Databases
Sergio Greco, Cristian Molinaro, and Francesca Spezzano
2012

Business Processes: A Database Perspective
Daniel Deutch and Tova Milo
2012

Data Protection from Insider Threats
Elisa Bertino
2012

Deep Web Query Interface Understanding and Integration
Eduard C. Dragut, Weiyi Meng, and Clement T. Yu
2012

P2P Techniques for Decentralized Applications
Esther Pacitti, Reza Akbarinia, and Manal El-Dick
2012

Query Answer Authentication
HweeHwa Pang and Kian-Lee Tan
2012

Declarative Networking
Boon Thau Loo and Wenchao Zhou
2012

Full-Text (Substring) Indexes in External Memory
Marina Barsky, Ulrike Stege, and Alex Thomo
2011

Spatial Data Management
Nikos Mamoulis
2011

Database Repairing and Consistent Query Answering
Leopoldo Bertossi
2011

Managing Event Information: Modeling, Retrieval, and Applications
Amarnath Gupta and Ramesh Jain
2011

Fundamentals of Physical Design and Query Compilation
David Toman and Grant Weddell
2011

Methods for Mining and Summarizing Text Conversations
Giuseppe Carenini, Gabriel Murray, and Raymond Ng
2011

Probabilistic Databases
Dan Suciu, Dan Olteanu, Christopher Ré, and Christoph Koch
2011

Peer-to-Peer Data Management
Karl Aberer
2011

Probabilistic Ranking Techniques in Relational Databases
Ihab F. Ilyas and Mohamed A. Soliman
2011

Uncertain Schema Matching
Avigdor Gal
2011

Fundamentals of Object Databases: Object-Oriented and Object-Relational Design
Suzanne W. Dietrich and Susan D. Urban
2010

Advanced Metasearch Engine Technology
Weiyi Meng and Clement T. Yu
2010

Web Page Recommendation Models: Theory and Algorithms
Sule Gündüz-Ögüdücü
2010

Multidimensional Databases and Data Warehousing
Christian S. Jensen, Torben Bach Pedersen, and Christian Thomsen
2010

Database Replication
Bettina Kemme, Ricardo Jimenez-Peris, and Marta Patino-Martinez
2010

Relational and XML Data Exchange
Marcelo Arenas, Pablo Barcelo, Leonid Libkin, and Filip Murlak
2010

User-Centered Data Management
Tiziana Catarci, Alan Dix, Stephen Kimani, and Giuseppe Santucci
2010

Data Stream Management
Lukasz Golab and M. Tamer Özsu
2010

Access Control in Data Management Systems
Elena Ferrari
2010

An Introduction to Duplicate Detection
Felix Naumann and Melanie Herschel
2010

Privacy-Preserving Data Publishing: An Overview
Raymond Chi-Wing Wong and Ada Wai-Chee Fu
2010

Keyword Search in Databases
Jeffrey Xu Yu, Lu Qin, and Lijun Chang
2009

Perspectives on Business Intelligence

Raymond T. Ng, Patricia C. Arocena, Denilson Barbosa, Giuseppe Carenini, Luiz Gomes, Jr., Stephan Jou, Rock Anthony Leung, Evangelos Milios, Renée J. Miller, John Mylopoulos, Rachel A. Pottinger, Frank Tompa, and Eric Yu

ISBN: 978-3-031-00720-0   paperback
ISBN: 978-3-031-01848-0   ebook

DOI 10.1007/978-3-031-01848-0

A Publication in the Springer series
SYNTHESIS LECTURES ON DATA MANAGEMENT

Lecture #32
Series Editor: M. Tamer Özsu, *University of Waterloo*
Series ISSN
Synthesis Lectures on Data Management
Print 2153-5418   Electronic 2153-5426

Perspectives on
Business Intelligence

Raymond T. Ng, Patricia C. Arocena, Denilson Barbosa, Giuseppe Carenini, Luiz
Gomes, Jr., Stephan Jou, Rock Anthony Leung, Evangelos Milios, Renée J. Miller,
John Mylopoulos, Rachel A. Pottinger, Frank Tompa, and Eric Yu

SYNTHESIS LECTURES ON DATA MANAGEMENT #32

ABSTRACT

In the 1980s, traditional Business Intelligence (BI) systems focused on the delivery of reports that describe the state of business activities in the past, such as for questions like "How did our sales perform during the last quarter?" A decade later, there was a shift to more interactive content that presented how the business was performing at the present time, answering questions like "How are we doing right now?" Today the focus of BI users are looking into the future. "Given what I did before and how I am currently doing this quarter, how will I do next quarter?"

Furthermore, fuelled by the demands of Big Data, BI systems are going through a time of incredible change. Predictive analytics, high volume data, unstructured data, social data, mobile, consumable analytics, and data visualization are all examples of demands and capabilities that have become critical within just the past few years, and are growing at an unprecedented pace.

This book introduces research problems and solutions on various aspects central to next-generation BI systems. It begins with a chapter on an industry perspective on how BI has evolved, and discusses how game-changing trends have drastically reshaped the landscape of BI. One of the game changers is the shift toward the consumerization of BI tools. As a result, for BI tools to be successfully used by business users (rather than IT departments), the tools need a business model, rather than a data model. One chapter of the book surveys four different types of business modeling. However, even with the existence of a business model for users to express queries, the data that can meet the needs are still captured within a data model. The next chapter on vivification addresses the problem of closing the gap, which is often significant, between the business and the data models. Moreover, Big Data forces BI systems to integrate and consolidate multiple, and often wildly different, data sources. One chapter gives an overview of several integration architectures for dealing with the challenges that need to be overcome.

While the book so far focuses on the usual structured relational data, the remaining chapters turn to unstructured data, an ever-increasing and important component of Big Data. One chapter on information extraction describes methods for dealing with the extraction of relations from free text and the web. Finally, BI users need tools to visualize and interpret new and complex types of information in a way that is compelling, intuitive, but accurate. The last chapter gives an overview of information visualization for decision support and text.

KEYWORDS

business intelligence, big data, business modeling, vivification, data integration, information extraction, information visualization

Contents

1 Introduction and the Changing Landscape of Business Intelligence 1

Stephan Jou and Raymond Ng

   1.1   Introduction 1

   1.2   The Role of Research and This Book 3

2 BI Game Changers: an Industry Viewpoint 7

Rock Leung, Chahab Nastar, Frederic Vanborre, Christophe Favart, Gregor Hackenbroich, Philip Taylor, and David Trastour

   2.1   Introduction 7

   2.2   Defining Business Intelligence 8

   2.3   Early Days of BI 9

   2.4   Classic BI 10

   2.5   Game-changing Trends 10

       2.5.1 Faster Business 11

       2.5.2 Bigger Data 13

       2.5.3 Better Software 14

   2.6   Next-generation BI 16

   2.7   Conclusions 17

3 Business Modeling for BI 19

Eric Yu, Jennifer Horkoff, John Mylopoulos, Gregory Richards, and Daniel Amyot

   3.1   Introduction 19

   3.2   Modeling Business Processes 20

   3.3   Strategic Business Modeling for Performance Management 22

   3.4   Modeling Business Models 24

   3.5   Toward Modeling for BI 28

       3.5.1 BIM Concepts 28

       3.5.2 Reasoning with BIM Models 30

   3.6   Conclusions 32

4   Vivification in BI **33**

Patricia C. Arocena, Renée J. Miller, and John Mylopoulos

4.1   Introduction 33

4.2   A Motivating Example 34

4.3   The Vivification Problem 37

    4.3.1   Knowledge Base Vivification 37

    4.3.2   Data Exchange 39

4.4   Formal Framework 40

4.5   Current Vivification Strategies 43

    4.5.1   Strategies for Dealing with Incompleteness 43

    4.5.2   Strategies for Dealing with Uncertainty 44

    4.5.3   Summary of Other Relevant Work 45

4.6   Toward Adaptive Vivification Strategies 46

    4.6.1   Vivification by Acceptance 46

    4.6.2   Vivification by Default 47

    4.6.3   Vivification by Resolution 48

4.7   Directions for Future Research 49

4.8   Conclusions 51

5   Information Integration in BI **53**

Rachel A. Pottinger

5.1   Introduction 53

5.2   Information Integration Goals and Axes 54

5.3   Challenges and Background 56

    5.3.1   Schemas and Semantic Heterogeneity 56

    5.3.2   Ontologies 57

5.4   Overview of Different Information Integration Architectures 57

    5.4.1   Data Integration 57

    5.4.2   Data Warehousing 61

    5.4.3   Peer Data Management Systems 64

5.5   Information Integration Tools in Industry 65

5.6   Conclusions 66

6   Information Extraction for BI **67**

Denilson Barbosa, Luiz Gomes, Jr., and Frank Wm. Tompa

6.1   Introduction 67

	6.1.1	Levels of Structuredness	68
	6.1.2	The Role of IE for BI	69
6.2		IE From Text	71
	6.2.1	Patterns in Language	72
	6.2.2	Named Entity Recognition	74
	6.2.3	Ontology Learning	79
	6.2.4	Relation Extraction	80
	6.2.5	Factoid Extraction	84
6.3		Data Extraction from the web	85
	6.3.1	Wrapper Induction	85
	6.3.2	Schema Extraction	86
6.4		BI over Raw Text	88
6.5		Conclusions	89

7 Information Visualization for BI **93**

Giuseppe Carenini and Evangelos Milios

7.1		Introduction	93
7.2		Information Visualization for Decision Support	93
	7.2.1	Information Visualization in the Performance Management Cycle: Information Dashboards	94
	7.2.2	Visualization for Preferential Choice	99
	7.2.3	Current and Future Trends in Information Visualization for Decision Support	103
7.3		Visualizing Text	105
	7.3.1	Text Clouds	105
	7.3.2	Topic Models	108
	7.3.3	Text Streams	109
	7.3.4	Sentiment Analytics	113
	7.3.5	Multiview Systems for Document Collections	117
7.4		Conclusions	123

Bibliography **125**

Authors' Biographies **145**

CHAPTER 1

Introduction and the Changing Landscape of Business Intelligence

Stephan Jou and Raymond Ng

1.1 INTRODUCTION

A lot has changed since 1958 when IBM researcher Hans Peter Luhn first coined the term Business Intelligence (BI) as "the ability to apprehend the interrelationships of presented facts in such a way as to guide action toward a desired goal" [Luhn, 1958]. In particular, the BI domain has seen dramatic changes in its use of temporal information, the nature of the data to analyze, cloud computing, user-centric and consumable analytics. All of these changes demand new, enabling research and technology capability that are exemplified by this book.

BI systems have traditionally focused on the delivery of reports that describe the state of business activities in the past. Questions like "How did our sales perform during the last quarter?" were answered through straightforward query generation and execution against structured and multidimensional data warehouses and delivered to end-users in a static report, such as a PDF document or simple web page.

In the 1990s, there was a shift from static reports of past performance to more interactive content that presented how the business was performing at the present time, answering questions like "How are we doing right now? This month, this day, this second?" This shift to real-time business intelligence was supported with new technologies: animated real-time dashboards, interactive filters, prompts, and multidimensional gestures augmented the classical, static content, while in-memory databases and other performance-enabling infrastructures surfaced.

Now the focus of business intelligence systems has shifted in the time domain yet again. In addition to asking questions about the past and the present, BI users are looking into the future. "Given what I did before and how I am currently doing this quarter, how will I do next quarter? How am I predicted to perform, and how does that compare to competitors who are in a similar situation? How can I tweak what I am doing right now to optimize my future?"

The addition of statistical and predictive analytical techniques—optimization, predictive modeling, simulation, and forecasting—to traditional BI methods—querying, reporting, and analysis—

has resulted in solutions that can predict and optimize the future. The development and incorporation of these future-facing technologies is one of the key events that strongly distinguishes classical business intelligence systems of the past from the new "business analytics and optimization" systems that have emerged from industry.

Dramatic changes have also occurred in the data and information that we now want to analyze. When BI systems were first adopted by industry, data warehouses were still being formed and sparsely populated, and therefore the BI technologies that emerged emphasized data collection and integration. The relational and OLAP databases held static snapshots of primarily numerical, very structured data held in well-defined schema. However, this picture has changed, and many in the industry today characterized the new data challenges with the "three V's" of volume, variety, and velocity.

These dramatic changes in data helped fuel the emergence and importance of enabling cloud computing technologies. In many ways, it was these new data demands that led to the development of our current ability to create and use virtualized computational, storage, analytical, and other infrastructural or platform services in various cloud environments.

Much of the new data of interest to businesses, particularly unstructured social data, comes from the Internet and was, therefore, "born" in the public cloud. At the same time, however, significant value continues to be extractable from data being generated or collected on-premise inside the corporate firewall, with potentially even greater value from the combination of both public and on-premise data. The large volume and high velocity nature of the data means copy operations from one location to another are impractical and sometimes impossible. As a result, it made sense to flexibly locate the systems required to analyze the data as close to its origins as possible, resulting in the development of public, on-premise (private), and hybrid cloud computing environments.

At the same time, analyzing the new varieties and large volumes of data requires significant computational power. The new predictive, text, and social analytics algorithms can sometimes require large numbers of computers—hundreds, thousands, even more—to work on the problem simultaneously in order to return a result with sufficient velocity. The rapid sequestration and orchestration of a large number of (virtual) computational and storage units for a relatively short period of time to perform these sorts of analyses cannot be practically done using traditional hardware infrastructure; a cloud computing infrastructure is the only cost-effective method of enabling this next generation of business analytics solutions.

Finally, the ability to programmatically define the deployed infrastructure in a cloud computing environment means that we can treat infrastructure as if it was software: we can algorithmically describe and tune the infrastructure to match the analysis we want to perform. This affords us tremendous flexibility and power compared to traditional BI infrastructure, allowing us to design large scale analytical solutions that were previously expensive or intractable.

Furthermore, traditional BI systems had a well-defined and controlled consumption model. IT specialists owned the data warehouses and the processes surrounding the data stored within those warehouses. Report authors created the reports and dashboards that consumed the data, and the resultant web pages or PDF files were delivered to BI end users. BI specialists created BI object models or predictive models to add semantics, rules, and predictive capabilities to the reports.

Now, the focus has definitely shifted from those specialized groups to the individual BI end users as the primary audience for the industry's next generation software. These new end users are very familiar with new technologies such as the Internet and mobile devices, and expect a level of interactivity, performance, and ease-of-use that traditional BI software has had to evolve and aspire to. They want to be able to analyze and combine the data that sits on their desktop files or that they have discovered on the Internet, and not just the enterprise data that has been made available to them by the IT specialists. They expect results in minutes to seconds, not hours to days. And finally, these end users might not have the training of a classical statistician, but they understand their business domain area completely and want to be able to perform deep predictive analyses themselves, without involving the BI specialists.

Building systems to enable these new user-centric and consumable analytics involves more than just recognizing the primacy of user experience and human-centric design to software, although that is certainly important. The challenges to supporting such systems range from infrastructural—how can we perform such difficult calculations quickly enough to power a responsive UI?—to conceptual—how can we bridge the modeling gap between database representation to the end user's business concepts—to representational—how can we visualize and represent information that is inherently complex in a way that is both consumable and accurate, without misleading the user unintentionally? The net result is a focus on user experiences that are powerfully intuitive while also being delightful, and a focus on methods to make very complex analytics usable, comprehensible, and consumable by the ordinary business user.

1.2   THE ROLE OF RESEARCH AND THIS BOOK

The business intelligence industry is going through a time of incredible change. Predictive analytics, high volume data, unstructured data, social data, mobile, consumable analytics, and data visualization are all examples of demands and capabilities that have become critical within just the past few years, and growing at an unprecedented pace.

This book introduces research problems and solutions on various aspects central to BI. The target audience of the book includes first-year graduate students and senior undergraduate students in Computer Science, and researchers and practitioners in either Computer Science or Business Administration.

Chapter 2 provides an industry perspective on how BI has evolved. It first describes the systems in early days of BI and classic BI. It then discusses how game-changing trends have drastically re-shaped the landscape of BI, with a projection into the future generation of BI tools. This sets up the rest of the book regarding ongoing research and development of BI tools.

One of the game changers is the shift toward the consumerization of BI tools. As a result, for BI tools to be successfully used by business users (rather than IT departments), the tools need to speak the language of the business user. However, a key problem with many existing BI tools is that they speak more an IT language than a business language. In other words, a data model is not what is useful to a user; rather, it is a business model that is needed. Chapter 3 surveys four different types of business modeling.

While the needs of a user are expressed in a business model, the data that can meet the needs are captured within a data model. There is a significant gap between the two models. Chapter 4 on vivification addresses the problem of bridging the gap between the two models. It discusses the development of mappings that connect the business schema with the database schema, and outlines various strategies for dealing with incompleteness and uncertainty that arise from the bridging process.

The trend toward bigger data forces our systems to integrate and consolidate multiple, and often wildly different, data sources. As a result, it is often the case that a business query requires data to be retrieved and integrated from multiple sources. Chapter 5 describes some of the challenges that need to be overcome, including schema and semantic heterogeneity and ontology integration. It gives an overview of several integration architectures for dealing with these challenges and for efficient query answering.

While the book so far focuses on the usual structured relational data, the remaining chapters of the book turn to unstructured data, an ever-increasing and important component of the bigger data trend. Chapter 6 on information extraction describes methods for dealing with the extraction of relations from free text, which may be embedded in web pages, emails, surveys, customer call records, etc.

Finally, addressing the demanding expectations of the new users of our BI solutions requires innovation and research in new ways of interacting with users to give them an interactive discovery and guided analysis process, of visualizing new and complex types of information in a way that is consumable, compelling, and delightful, but also accurate. The last chapter of the book presents tools for visualizing text in data, as well as general visualization tools for BI users.

The topics selected for this book are aligned with the research done by collaborators within the pan-Canada Business Intelligence Network funded by the Natural Sciences and Engineering Research Council of Canada. To create an innovation platform for pre-competitive BI research within Canada, the network aims to enhance Canadian business competitiveness through the development of intelligent data management and decision-making solutions. The authors of this book are all network participants.

Note that the network includes many research projects not covered by the chapters in this book. Two notable omissions are data cleansing and cloud computing. Different data sources, particularly social data, also imply different levels of trust than the traditional "clean" data found in a data warehouse. The question of how to cleanse data from these new and complex data sources is an important research direction. Within the Synthesis Lectures on Data Management series, the reader is referred to the lecture by Bertossi [2011], which addresses some of the data cleansing issues encountered in BI systems. Within the same series, the lecture by Deutch and Milo [2012] addresses modeling and querying of business processes beyond the discussion in Chapter 3. And the lecture by Carenini et al. [2011] considers information extraction beyond what is discussed in Chapter 6. Last but not least, the article by Armbrust et al. [2010] provides a comprehensive overview on cloud computing. We refer the interested reader to the aforementioned papers for more details on these topics.

CHAPTER 2

BI Game Changers: an Industry Viewpoint

Rock Leung, Chahab Nastar, Frederic Vanborre, Christophe Favart, Gregor Hackenbroich, Philip Taylor, and David Trastour

2.1 INTRODUCTION

To compete in today's markets, business users need to effectively use a large volume of data to make strategic and efficient decisions to help a business meet its goals. With the decreasing price of computer data storage, businesses are collecting and storing more business data at a greater detail. However, the increasingly large amounts of data are becoming more difficult to access and analyze, in part because the data are often stored in a variety of data formats in a variety of storage systems. Thus, despite the investments in storing business data, a recent survey by BusinessWeek [Hammond, 2004] found that a majority of the business users today are still going on "gut feel," and not utilizing the data from these systems to make effective business decisions. Researchers of this survey found that only one fifth of respondents say they always have the right amount of information to make an informed business decision, and over three quarters were aware of situations where managers made bad business decisions because these managers did not have sufficient information.

BI technologies, especially Business Analytics (more detailed definitions to be given later), are designed to empower business users to more efficiently make sense of vast amounts of data and make better decisions. Businesses are increasingly investing in BI software and the effective use of BI is seen as a competitive advantage. Business Analytics software is forecasted to grow faster than the overall enterprise software market [Vesset et al., 2010].

Although past and current BI solutions have helped business users, these are evolving rapidly to meet new business needs and incorporate recent technological advances. These business and technological trends present many opportunities for next generation BI technologies to better support business users. Pursuing these opportunities also raises many new research questions about how to make effective use of these new technologies. For example, how can BI systems make better use of artificial intelligence, social networks, or mobile computing devices to better support the business user?

In this chapter we discuss recent changes in Business Intelligence from our viewpoint as industrial researchers. Our team, the Business Intelligence Practice, is a group in SAP Research that focuses on exploring the use of new technologies in next generation BI systems. As part of SAP, a market leader in enterprise application software, we are exposed to BI market trends, as well as the needs of large and small businesses. Further, we continually collaborate with academia with expertise in a variety of research areas such as text analytics, predictive analytics, visual analytics, semantic mashup, enterprise search, and collaborative decision making.

We begin this chapter by defining BI in context of business data and business users' actions. We then describe past and current BI systems and how they support the business user. The section that follows discusses many new business needs and technology trends that have contributed to the evolution of the BI. We then present our vision of the next generation of BI systems. Although we refer to businesses throughout the chapter, many of our claims also generalize to other organizations including non-profit organizations.

Through this chapter, we hope to make two contributions. First, we summarize how BI systems have evolved and share our vision on what the next generation of BI will look like. Second, we hope to help academic and industry researchers position their research work in the new view of BI and focus on research questions that are the most relevant to today's BI challenges.

2.2   DEFINING BUSINESS INTELLIGENCE

While there are varying definitions for *BI*, Forrester defines it broadly as a "set of methodologies, processes, architectures, and technologies that transform raw data into meaningful and useful information [that] allows business users to make informed business decisions with real-time data that can put a company ahead of its competitors" [Evelson, 2008]. In other words, the high-level goal of BI is to help a business user turn business-related data into actionable knowledge. BI traditionally focused on reports, dashboards, and answering predefined questions [Beller and Barnett, 2009]. Today BI also includes a focus on deeper, exploratory, and interactive analyses of the data using *Business Analytics* such as data mining, predictive analytics, statistical analysis, and natural language processing solutions [Evelson, 2008].

Consider the following cycle shown in Figure 2.1 involving a business user and her business's data. Starting from the *data* circle (Figure 2.1, bottom circle), the user accesses enterprise data such as financial transactions (e.g., "$19.99," "2," "21432"), which is generated and stored by the business. To begin making sense of this data, semantics are added to turn the data into more useful *information* (e.g., "2 shirts (product ID 21432) were bought at $19.99 each"). To analyze this information, a business user (e.g., store manager, another analyst) can choose, or be presented with, information that is relevant, trustworthy, and suitably presented for her purposes, in order to generate higher-level *knowledge* (e.g., whether her past actions/strategy helped her meet a monthly revenue goal).

The business user then interprets the knowledge gained from the data to determine what to do next. Specifically, the user has goals associated with her job (e.g., monthly revenue target), and one or more strategies to meet those goals (e.g., increase sales volume for popular products). The user can determine from the data whether the goals are being met and whether strategies are working. Continuing her data analysis and then weighing various options, the user *decides* what actions that she would like to take (e.g., offer discounts, advertise product). The *actions* within the user's means are executed (e.g., discount product ID 21432), which the user hopes will have a positive impact on business but will need to confirm later by analyzing future data.

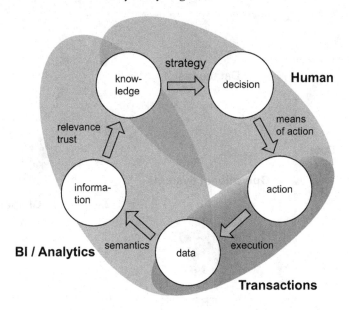

Figure 2.1: The virtuous cycle of business data

In the cycle of business data, BI (Figure 2.1, blue oval) is used to transform data to information to knowledge that the business user can then act on. In other words, BI takes a wide variety of high-dimensional, low-semantics data and refines the data into low-dimensional knowledge with high-semantics (i.e., fewer but more useful dimensions).

The development of BI systems taps several research and development areas. BI draws from work in databases to ensure, for example, that large volumes of business data are easily accessible, have minimal errors, and can be combined with different sources. BI also draws from work in data mining, text analysis, semantic analysis, and many other research areas that transform data into information. Further, BI draws from areas such as human-computer interaction, information visualization, and other areas that help the business user analyze, explore, and create knowledge from the information derived from business data. BI technologies also draw from work in networking and computer architectures.

2.3   EARLY DAYS OF BI

In the early days of BI, business data were stored in traditional databases, as shown in Figure 2.2. Data consisted of operational systems data and Enterprise Resource Planning (ERP) data. Accessing the data and processing it to a more consumable form required the IT and analytical skills of an IT specialist. Thus, the business user needed to go through an IT specialist to access and analyze the business data. The turnaround between posing a business question to getting an answer often took weeks.

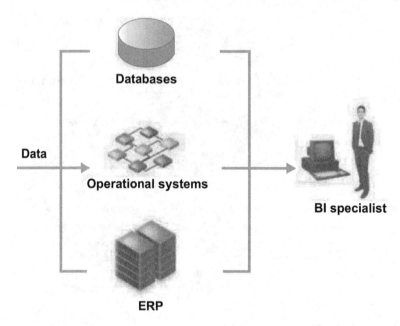

Figure 2.2: BI systems in the "early days."

2.4   CLASSIC BI

In the early 1990s, BI systems evolved into what we call Classic BI by adding layers of data "staging" to increase the accessibility of the business data to business users. Data from the operational systems and ERP were extracted, transformed into a more consumable form (e.g., column names labeled for human rather than computer consumption, errors corrected, duplication eliminated). Data from a warehouse were then loaded into OLAP cubes, as well as data marts stored in data warehouses. OLAP cubes facilitated the analysis of data over several dimensions. Data marts present a subset of the data in the warehouse, tailored to a specific line of business. Using classic BI, the business user, with the help of an IT specialist who had set up the system for her, could now more easily access and analyze the data through a BI system.

2.5   GAME-CHANGING TRENDS

A number of game-changing trends have recently emerged that we believe will significantly transform how BI is used, and affect the way product developers and researchers need to look at BI. We believe

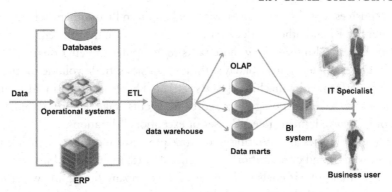

Figure 2.3: Classic BI system.

that BI, particularly Business Analytics, is at a tipping point in terms of its complexity, sophistication, and ease-of-use. These trends not only require new and advanced BI tools, but also raise new exciting research questions for industry and academic researchers to tackle.

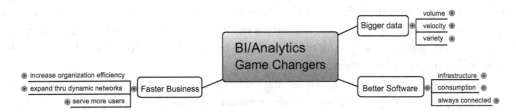

Figure 2.4: Game changing trends in Business Intelligence

2.5.1   FASTER BUSINESS

To stay competitive, businesses need to be as efficient as possible, be more innovative through dynamic networks, and serve more users.

Increasing Organization Efficiency

Businesses are empowering their employees to help them more independently make better and faster decisions. Businesses are working toward giving their employees access to the business data they need, when they need it, to help them perform their job effectively. This applies to employees at all levels, from top executives to those directly supporting customers. While business users often work at a desktop computer, there is also a need to support these users when they are in other settings such as meeting rooms, their commutes, and at the customer site. Thus, BI systems that support collaboration and mobile computing are needed. In addition, having business users access and analyze business data by themselves, without help from IT or others helps to increase efficiency. Thus, self-service BI and other work systems can also increase the efficiency of the business.

Businesses are also delegating more tasks to computers, freeing their employees to focus on other work. For example, approximately a third of all stock trade volume on the New York Stock Exchange are performed by machines [EDN, 2012]. There is a trend in BI, which is common in other domains, to have technology (e.g., software agents) take actions automatically in "normal" cases and only involve humans in edge cases or exceptional situations.

Further, businesses are adopting new work processes to empower their employees and improve responsiveness and organizational efficiency. For example, many businesses are helping their employees better align their goals with those of the company through new performance management tools such as Key Performance Indicators and Management by Objectives. Businesses are also adopting agile product development processes (e.g., scrum, lean) in order to help employees work more efficiently together.

Innovation through Dynamic Networks

Businesses need to innovate to compete, but they often cannot rely on internal research and development to sustain the pace of innovation desired by businesses. We are seeing an increased desire by businesses to innovate with other organizations, as well as end users, through dynamic networks. Many businesses are using an open innovation model to work with other companies and academic researchers to generate and productize ideas [Chesbrough et al., 2006]. The NSERC BI Network exemplifies this open innovation model.

New business models are also emerging that require more powerful business analytics for guidance. Many businesses, particularly technology-producing ones, are adopting models like "freemium" and ad-powered models. Others are focused on selling to the "Long Tail," building a large number of products or services, each being bought at relatively small quantities but collectively total a large quantity. Thus, many businesses have a relatively larger and more diverse customer (and potential customer) base that they need to analyze and track. Understanding, serving, and selling to this customer base requires more powerful business analytics.

Serving More Users

BI systems are increasingly being used by end users and operational business users, and not only analysts. Thus, the next generation of BI systems needs to be designed for people who have less experience with analytical tools and less training on these systems.

Given the increasing number of networked computational devices (e.g., laptops, smart phones, tablets) it is increasingly more feasible for a business to reach more users. SAP, for example, wants to increase the number of SAP software users from millions of users to 1 billion users by 2015. Reaching more users requires better understanding a variety of target users, their needs, and how they use their devices.

2.5.2   BIGGER DATA

The cost of acquiring and storing data has declined significantly and thus businesses increasingly want to analyze more data (i.e., Big Data) to remain competitive. Big Data has often been characterized by increased volume, velocity, and variety [Russom, 2011]. We discuss each of these three dimensions below.

Volume

Like most digital data, the volume of business data is increasing over time. Businesses want to capture data in greater detail, in order to uncover more insights. As businesses rely more on computers for conducting business, data are being generated by more computer users, such as business employees and customers. Data are also generated by the increasing number of powerful mobile computing devices (e.g., smart phones, tablets), and connected sensors (e.g., Internet of Things). The amount of world's digital information data doubles every 18 month. What tools are needed to help business users manage and analyze huge volumes of data?

Velocity

Business data are also being collected at a greater rate. Business users also want to reduce the time it takes to answer a question, ideally in real time. In the early days of BI, analyzing enterprise data for a particular business question often took several days. In those days, reporting and analysis was often done in batches. Technology has enabled businesses to reduce the time it takes to access and process their data. Current BI systems are allowing businesses to analyze their data in "near real-time." Future BI systems will one day support real-time analysis of business data, and analysis of data streams. What tools are needed to help business users process increasingly greater rates of business data generation?

Variety

A business's enterprise data are traditionally structured, trusted, internal, and based on objective facts. However, businesses would now like to analyze a wider variety of data to discover additional insights. The variety of data that businesses are interested in analyzing can be categorized according to the following dimensions:

- *Structured/unstructured*: Enterprise data include data that are generally structured in a set of well-defined fields, and is typically stored in tables. Enterprise data can also consist of unstructured data (e.g., content of a text document, video content) that often have to be mined or modeled in order to extract meaningful information.

- *Trusted/non-certified*: Data can come from a variety of sources. Data can come from a trusted source (e.g., generated within the business). Enterprise data are generally trusted by the business, especially after the data are cleaned (e.g., data from a data warehouse). Data can also come from an external source and its accuracy, completeness, objectivity may not be certain. Online data (e.g., databases available for free on the Internet) are generally considered non-certified, at least initially. A set of data can move along this trustedness dimension; for example, the data can be more trustworthy if the data are consistent with other trusted data or if other data from the same source are found to be trustworthy.

- *Internal/external*: Data can be generated within an organization or externally. Businesses have traditionally focused on analyzing internally generated business data. However, enterprise processes are now distributed and much of the business data will be collected outside the company's walls. For example, businesses often rely on a supply chain consisting of partners and suppliers, and an ecosystem of sellers. Some businesses use GPS truck monitoring to evaluate the provisioning chain and optimize production and/or product delivery. In addition, businesses are increasingly interested in analyzing online social networks and product review websites, generally externally hosted, to better understand consumer behaviours and market trends.

- *Facts/opinions*: Business data are generally facts (e.g., financial transactions, number of hours worked), but business data can also consist of opinions (e.g., employee satisfaction, customer ratings on a product).

Analyzing a wider variety of data requires new tools and techniques to combine, as well as differentiate, different types of data. How can tools allow users to easily analyze different types of data together? How can these tools also help users differentiate between the two types of data when analyzing them together?

2.5.3   BETTER SOFTWARE

Major technological advances in computer software and hardware have also provided opportunities to meet many needs related to faster businesses and processing Big Data. There are three advances that are particularly relevant for BI: infrastructure, data and software consumption, and increased connectedness.

Infrastructure

BI systems are incorporating cloud technologies, which are changing the way BI is deployed. Enterprise technology has historically been deployed "on premise" at the customer's site. However, BI technologies are now being offered as a service through the cloud, providing increased scalability, connectedness, and ease of deployment. Cloud technologies provide businesses more agility and flexibility in their IT systems to scale on demand. These technologies are also always on, which is crucial for online and mobile services to end users. Further, cloud technologies enable customers to use new BI systems sooner, without the need for upfront deployments of servers and software.

Advances in database technology have increased the business user's ability to quickly analyze data. In-memory technologies allow entire databases to reside in a server's memory instead of relatively slower disk storage, speeding up database accesses by orders of magnitude [Plattner, 2009,

Plattner and Zeier, 2011]. This technology has been found to be well suited for structured data and real-time processing. What other data processing and analysis can in-memory technologies help speed up?

Advances in distributed computing have increased a business's ability to store and process very large volumes of data. For example, the Apache Hadoop software framework, consisting of the Hadoop distributed File System and MapReduce distributed computing engine, can store and process petabytes of data [Apache, 2011]. Hadoop has been found to be suited for large volumes of data, unstructured data, and batch processing.

Consumption

Enterprise software has traditionally been data-centric, but this software is moving toward being more user-centric. In fact, enterprise software is lagging behind consumer software on this front, and there's a clear need to "consumerize" enterprise software [Moore, 2011].

How can enterprise software be designed to be easier for users to consume? Business users are generally consumers of other technologies (e.g., smart phones, Internet search engines, social networks, and computer games) so enterprise software may benefit from incorporating the many new features and intuitive interaction methods used on those technologies. Researchers are also exploring how "gamifying" enterprise software can help ease consumption by adding game elements to motivate engagement and help users learn to perform initial tasks and then more advanced tasks [Burke and Hiltbrand, 2011]. Tailoring the user experience for each individual user or small demographics may also make the software easier to consume. Personalizing the user experience requires measuring and making effective use of contextual data (e.g., a user's location, organizational role, current task, previous tasks). Social networks also enable users to collaboratively consume data and make decisions as a group.

Businesses also need new tools to consume Big Data. For example, new analytical tools like Visual Analytics applications are needed to explore large volumes of data. As another example, new tools are needed to process the wide variety of data a business user is interested in. Structured data have traditionally been accessed by business users through database queries. In contrast, text and multimedia content have traditionally been accessed through searching on keywords. The frontiers between structured data and content are now quickly vanishing and the business user wants to search many different types of data through one information retrieval tool such as the familiar search input text field (e.g., Google Search, Bing). Moreover, business data are not only consumed by business users but by machines as well. How can we design BI tools to make use of machine-to-machine data?

Increased Connectedness

Business users are increasingly connected through technology. For example, the latest mobile phones enable users to remotely communicate and collaborate more with others. Business users are now able to access their business's data in order to make better decisions away from their desk (e.g., customer site, manufacturing plant, while commuting). To make better use of BI through mobile devices, researchers are exploring how to personalize the data and user experience. How can we make use of the user's position in the company, access to data, task, location, and other contextual information to personalize their experience?

Many businesses are interested in making use of social networks. Social networks enable users to engage with other individuals, groups, and communities. Using social networks, businesses can tap into both the wisdom of the crowd, as well as the network of experts. Social network can also be used to evaluate partners, suppliers, products, potential recruits, and co-workers. How can social networks and online collaboration tools be used to support decision making? How can these technologies help business users analyze data?

More devices and sensors are being connected to the Internet (e.g., Internet of Things). The Internet of Things can be thought of as an automated part of collecting insights. Data from sensors such as RFID tags for goods, GPS tracking for trucks, gate control for building's entrance, and building's temperature sensors can be used to answer business questions and provide actionable insights for a whole company, a product team, or an individual employee.

2.6   NEXT-GENERATION BI

Given the many game changes in BI that were described in the earlier section, we predict that the next generation BI software will include evolutions in both hardware infrastructure and data processing. As stated earlier, new advanced infrastructures will change how much data is stored and how quickly we can access large amounts of it (see Figure 2.5). Instead of using traditional relational databases, a business can use distributed storage systems such as Hadoop to store data warehouses and large volumes of other data that the business wants to analyze. In-memory technologies (e.g., SAP HANA, IBM solidDB, Oracle TimesTen) will allow business users to execute data queries thousands of times faster than current generation systems, greatly increasing the volume of data that can be analyzed at once as well as the interactivity of the analytical tool. We envision the distributed storage/computing system integrating the data sources and feeding the in-memory technology. The analytics will access the in-memory or distributed computing system as needed.

Next-generation BI systems will also allow users to process greater varieties of data and produce better insights from it. As mentioned earlier, the goal of BI is to refine all kinds of high-dimensional, low-semantics data and to present low-dimensional knowledge with high-semantics to the end user. BI systems traditionally only enabled the analysis of structured business data (e.g., financial transaction) but new systems will analyze many more types of data. As shown in Figure 2.6, next-generation BI systems will also process multimedia content (e.g., video, image, sound), text content, data steams (e.g., RSS, logs, device sensor data, smart items), and graphs, often together with structured data.

These various types of data are stored in a knowledge base that pushes the data to the user and enables the business user to pull data from the knowledge base (see Figure 2.6). The data can be pushed to the user through personalized (i.e., contextual, recommended) dashboards and alerts. The

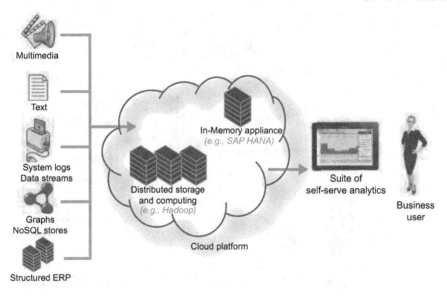

Figure 2.5: Our vision for the next-generation BI system.

user can also pull the data through reports, queries/searches, and data exploration. These systems will be designed to support self-service, enabling the business user to analyze data with little assistance from IT specialists (see Figure 2.5).

BI systems will also have a "control loop" in which data can be written-back to the data sources or knowledge database. This write-back can be done explicitly by the user, say to correct or annotate the data. The BI system can also record the user's behaviour or status (e.g., geo-location, query logs) in the data sources, to provide additional contextual data for future personalized presentation or data analysis. Furthermore, there may be a loop in which a machine makes decisions on the users' behalf (e.g., using business rules) and the business user is not directly involved.

2.7   CONCLUSIONS

Businesses are relying increasingly on Business Intelligence to remain competitive in their market. Past BI systems have allowed business users to access and analyze business data with the help of an IT specialist. Current BI systems reduce the dependency on an IT specialist, and help users make better sense of their data. We listed a number of new business needs and technology trends that both require, and help to develop, next-generation BI systems. New BI systems will allow business users to analyze a larger volume, increased velocity, and wider variety of data, with minimal involvement from IT.

This is an exciting time for BI research, as there are many opportunities to develop more powerful and easy-to-use analytical tools for business users. We have listed a few of the many

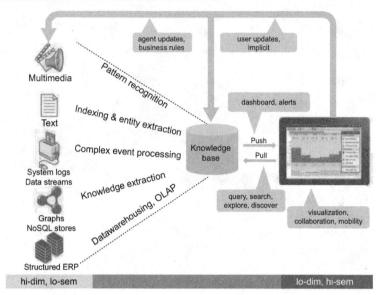

Figure 2.6: Processing new types of data.

research questions that need to be explored to continue advancing BI and realize the next-generation BI systems. Next-generation BI will enable businesses and other organizations to gain more insights from their data and make better decisions.

CHAPTER 3

Business Modeling for BI

Eric Yu, Jennifer Horkoff, John Mylopoulos, Gregory Richards, and Daniel Amyot

3.1 INTRODUCTION

BI is becoming ever more woven into the fabric of organizations today, particularly those dealing with large amounts of data. Retailers are using BI to analyze consumer tastes and purchase patterns, to optimize supply chains, and to plan product strategies and campaigns. Mobile providers use BI to monitor customer sentiments, anticipate churn, and to map the competitive landscape. In healthcare, BI is being used to evaluate drug effectiveness, reduce wait times, and improve quality of care. Government agencies use BI to uncover wastage and opportunities for reducing costs and improving services. In the energy and environmental sectors, BI and big data analytics are crucial in the drive for sustainability. In all of these settings, successful deployment of BI relies on a proper understanding of the business domain. The better the BI system reflects the mental model of its users, the more value it can provide.

In information systems engineering, conceptual modeling at the business level aims to provide languages, notations, methodologies, and tools for expressing knowledge about business domains so that IT systems will accurately and effectively support business objectives. Conceptual models provide clear and concise understanding of a domain by building upon a (usually small) set of fundamental concepts that are essential for describing and analyzing the domain. The challenge is to find a set of concepts that are sufficiently expressive (allowing the user to say what she wants about the domain), have good reasoning support (to do analysis and inference), yet simple enough for the intended user community. Concepts found to be fundamental for information system applications include the following aspects or dimensions [Mylopoulos, 1998]:

- The static aspect—objects or entities and their relationships

- The dynamic aspect—activities, processes, states and transitions

- The intentional aspect—intent, goals, objectives, rationales, choices, trade-offs, etc.

- The social aspect—actors, stakeholders, roles, etc.

A large number of modeling languages and techniques have been devised to address these aspects in various ways and in different combinations. However, the vast majority of them are meant to be used in the context of developing information systems that automate business operations. Conceptual modeling at the business level from a BI perspective remains a wide-open research area.

Conceptual modeling for BI will need to consider the perspectives of different types of users and usage contexts. Senior executives will want to assemble data from across the enterprise to assess performance and to develop strategy. Business strategists will want to monitor the competitive landscape, recognize threats and opportunities, to leverage strengths and exploit weaknesses. Business units will want to optimize operational processes and meet objectives. Frontline personnel can provide better service by having up-to-the-minute personalized information about specific customers. What concepts and languages are suitable for each of these classes of users to think about and work with the vast volumes of data that can now be at their fingertips through the latest BI technologies? What kinds of questions would they ask? How would they frame their questions? These are research questions for business modeling.

In the next sections, we sample four kinds of business modeling. In Section 3.2, we briefly review business process modeling, which is well established in information systems engineering. In Section 3.3, we consider strategy mapping for performance management, which is widely used in the business world. In Section 3.4, we consider the modeling of business models, as the Internet has triggered business model innovation in many sectors. Finally, in Section 3.5, we consider a modeling language meant to address the specific needs of BI.

3.2   MODELING BUSINESS PROCESSES

Business processes constitute the backbone of most business operations, and therefore figure prominently in any in-depth understanding of a business. Processes crosscut an organization in many ways, connecting human and automated activities to create value for external customers or stakeholders. A great deal of data for business intelligence originates from business processes. Models of business processes are therefore crucial not only in process design, but also in understanding how to collect data for BI.

Figure 3.1 shows a portion of a sales process modeled in the Business Process Model and Notation (BPMN) [White and Miers, 2008]. Activities are connected by sequence flows (solid arrows) as well as data flows (dashed arrows). Branching can be conditional on data or events. Swimlanes are used to organize different units of responsibility.

Aside from depicting the main business activities of payment, checkout, and delivery, this example illustrates how BI processing steps (the bottom two swimlanes—for spool and daily revenue) can be included in the same model, thus helping analyze how BI can augment the business process. This kind of analysis is particularly relevant as BI is increasingly incorporated into operational processes (sometimes called operational BI, in contrast to BI for analyzing historical data). In the example, the company wants to make special offers to particular customers based on their purchasing history, recent browsing actions, today's revenue, and current inventory. This operation requires data from Online Transaction Processing (OLTP) databases, the data warehouse, as well as in-flight data that may be on the way to the data warehouse. Dayal et al. [2009] explain how modeling at

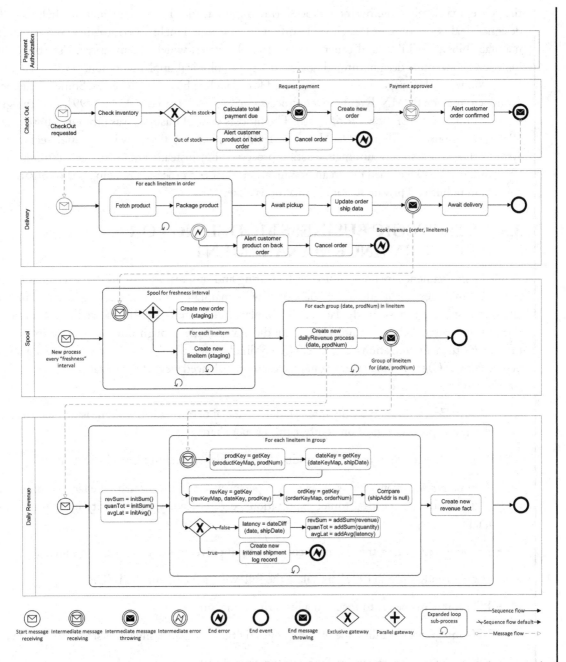

Figure 3.1: Business process (check out, delivery) augmented with BI process (spool, daily revenue) (from [Dayal et al., 2009]).

the conceptual level of the business process (in contrast to the IT implementation) helps the BI designer deal with complex design trade-offs involving functionality, performance, recoverability, maintainability, reliability, and other service level objectives, which are manifested starting from high-level conceptual design, through logical design, to physical implementation.

Numerous languages have been proposed for modeling business processes. Some of the most prominent include BPMN, Event-driven Process Chain (EPC) [van der Aalst, 1999], and (Integration DEFinition) IDEF (www.idef.com). The process view of business was promoted in the early 1990s [Davenport and Short, 1990, Hammer, 1990] emphasizing that new information technology systems should not simply automate existing processes, but instead should trigger a rethinking of how work can best be carried out in an organization. Business processes remain a major organizing concept in public and private sector organizations alike.

3.3   STRATEGIC BUSINESS MODELING FOR PERFORMANCE MANAGEMENT

While IT departments are preoccupied with creating and supporting systems that execute business processes, management needs to be concerned with maintaining and improving performance in all aspects of the business. In the late 1980s, Kaplan and Norton [1992] observed that traditional financial measures such as earnings per share did not provide enough information for executives to manage their organizations effectively. Accordingly, they developed the concept of Balanced Scorecards (BSC) so that managers would have a more balanced view of organizational performance covering four perspectives:

- *Shareholders*, who are typically interested in financial performance, with measures such as cash flow, sales growth, return on equity, earnings per share.

- *Customers*, who are interested in product/service quality, lead times, and so forth.

- *Internal process*, an operations management perspective often focused on the factors companies must excel at to meet customer expectations, e.g., efficiency, productivity cycle times, and quality.

- *Learning and growth*, the ability to continue to improve, innovate, and create value.

  Kaplan and Norton [1992] articulate the following benefits for the BSC:

- BSC forces managers to focus on a few critical measures;

- BSC integrates the full scope of company activities into one easily understood dashboard;

- BSC provides a holistic view of the organization, therefore avoiding the achievement of results in one area at the expense of another; and

- BSC emphasizes strategy and vision as opposed to control.

The BSC concept was further developed into a visual graphical model linking the four areas of performance, called strategy maps by Kaplan and Norton [2000]. A strategy map shows layers of objectives defined by managers for each perspective. A strategy here refers to a particular way of getting something done. For example, "investing in new product development" might be one strategy for achieving the strategic objective of "grow market share by 20%."

The objectives are defined in a top-down manner. Objectives higher in the map are defined first. Objectives at lower levels are then identified as drivers for the higher-level objectives. Figure 3.2 provides a simplified example of a strategy map (showing only a single objective at each layer).

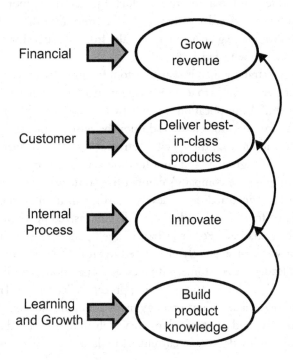

Figure 3.2: Simplified Strategy Map–Product Leadership.

In this example, company managers would have already defined the product-market focus and articulated a specific revenue growth target. The strategy map indicates that the best way to grow revenue is to deliver best-in-class products because this is what the market segment needs. Therefore, this company must excel at innovation. This objective is noted in the Internal Process perspective. Innovation, in turn, depends on building product knowledge among company staff, an objective reflected in the Learning and Growth perspective. The curved arrows in Figure 3.1 reflect the overall logic of the map. Reading from the bottom up, these arrows indicate that investments in product knowledge lead to innovation that leads to best-in-class products that, in turn, leads to revenue growth.

This particular map, therefore, reflects a "product leadership" competitive strategy. Clearly, the company also has to be able to manufacture and deliver products at a reasonable price, but the emphasis would be on ensuring the development of high quality, innovative products.

Managers would complete the map by adding performance measures for each objective (in some cases, more than one measure might be used). These measures serve a number of critical performance management purposes. First, they allow managers to monitor accomplishment of objectives in each perspective. Second, they help focus operational activities on the product leadership strategy. Third, they can be used to test the logic of the map itself. For example, the strategy hypothesizes that customers would respond to innovative products by purchasing more products or by purchasing newer products at a higher price. By gathering performance measures describing trends in product sales and product innovation (e.g., percentage of sales from products introduced within the past two years), this hypothesis can be tested.

In summary, the strategy map is seen as a tool for strategic execution: specific objectives and measures in each perspective helps to focus management attention on key activities needed to deliver on the strategy adopted. The implication is that activities that are "off strategy" should be eliminated thus improving organizational efficiency. In addition, because the measures attached to each objective allow for continuous monitoring, the specific activities that lead to success can be identified. The map therefore promotes alignment and coordination across the organization ostensibly leading to more effective execution of the company's competitive strategy.

Strategies can be defined at different levels in an organization. At the enterprise level, corporate strategy is often related to product-market focus. In contrast, competitive strategy is typically about how to win in selected markets. Porter [1980] defined generic competitive strategies (cost versus differentiation) that were subsequently elaborated upon by Treacy and Wiersema [1997] as value disciplines: product leadership, customer intimacy, and operational excellence. Kaplan and Norton's 2000 article that described the strategy mapping process relied on the Treacy and Wiersema value discipline framework to articulate how strategy maps communicate competitive strategy.

Balanced Scorecard and Strategy Maps are widely understood and used in the business world, and are supported to varying degrees in current BI tools.

3.4   MODELING BUSINESS MODELS

A *business model* describes how a business enterprise creates, delivers and captures value [Osterwalder and Pigneur, 2009]. Value is delivered through products and services offered by the enterprise. The business model describes then what these products and services are, for what market segments they are intended, through what channels they are to be delivered and at what price. It also describes the network of partners to be used to produce and deliver value.

Business models offer a complementary perspective to strategic models (that focus on objectives), structural/organizational models (that focus on the structure of an enterprise), and process models that focus on the processes through which an enterprise conducts its business.

There have been many proposals for classifying enterprises according to their business model type. For example, Weill et al. [2005] classify business models along two dimensions. The first considers the kinds of rights being sold. For example, a company may be selling *ownership* (e.g., Amazon.com selling ownership of books), or the *right-to-use* (Avis renting you a car for the weekend). Alternatively, a company may be selling the right to be matched, as with a real estate agency. The authors add to these three categories a fourth: enterprises that significantly alter the assets they sell. This category is introduced to distinguish between manufacturers and distributors. The second dimension considers the kinds of assets being sold: physical (a book), financial (a mortgage), intangible (a patent), or human (a person's time and/or expertise).

Given the complementary perspective relative to other kinds of enterprise models, we now examine the primitive concepts in terms of which one constructs business models, i.e., what concepts should be included in a language for expressing (modeling) business models (Figure 3.3). The concepts we present were proposed in the doctoral dissertation of Osterwalder [2004], and they are intended to serve as primitive terms for answering nine questions: (i) What do we offer to our customers? (ii) Who are our customers? (iii) How do we reach them? (iv) How do we get and keep them? (v) What are our revenues? Our pricing? (vi) What are our costs? (vii) How do we operate and deliver? (viii) How do we collaborate? (ix) What are our key competencies?

Question (i) is answered in terms of *value propositions*. A value proposition is a bundle of offerings that together represent value for potential customers. For an (imaginary) Italian ice cream company, 'ice cream' is a primary value proposition, refined into 'ice cream cone' and 'ice cream by the kilo'.

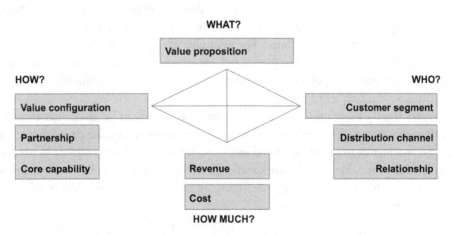

Figure 3.3: Primitive concepts for business models.

The concepts of *customer segment*, *distribution channel*, and *customer relationship* are introduced to answer questions (ii) to (iv). A customer segment describes the kinds of customers for which a value proposition is intended. For example, the general public includes all possible customers, while students is a specific kind of customer with respect to age and occupation that a value proposition such as ice cream cones may be aimed at. A store constitutes a distribution channel for a company that wants to get in touch with its customers. An ice cream cart is a more specialized distribution channel that can bring a value proposition to places frequented by a particular customer segment, e.g., schools for students. Finally, customer relationship describes the means by which customers are acquired and retained. Such mechanisms may be based on trust, brand recognition, personalization, etc. For instance, personalization is important for neighborhood stores and ice cream carts, while brand recognition plays a big role for mass customer segments.

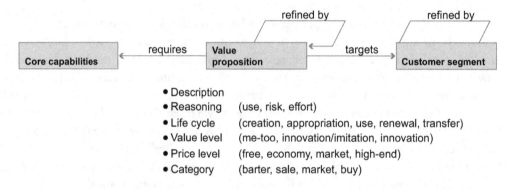

Figure 3.4: Associations and attributes for value propositions.

Figure 3.4 provides additional information about value propositions. In particular, each value proposition requires certain capabilities and targets one or more market segments. Value propositions and customer segments can be refined. For example, 'ice cream' may be refined into 'ice cream by the kilo,' sold through supermarket stores, and 'ice cream cone' sold via ice cream stores and carts. Likewise the general public as a customer segment can be refined into students, elderly, or workers (e.g., customer who frequent a factory plant).

Apart from a description, each value proposition needs to be associated through attributes with other information. For example, how do we judge a particular value proposition (reasoning), in terms of demand, risk in producing it and selling it, or the effort/cost involved? What is the lifecycle state of a value proposition, initiation (creation), use, renewal, etc.? What is its value level? Are we just copying a competitor (me-too), or offering an innovative product? What price level have we decided on: free, economy, high-end, …?

Figure 3.5 illustrates uses of the concepts introduced above for the Italian ice cream example, along with the inter-relationships among value propositions, distribution channels, and customer segments.

Value configurations, *partnerships*, and *capabilities* are key concepts for answering questions (vii) to (ix). A value configuration is a collection of activities that creates value. For example, the processes by which the ice cream company makes ice cream is one (basic) value configuration. Of course, a value configuration requires resources, such as the ingredients to be used for the ice cream

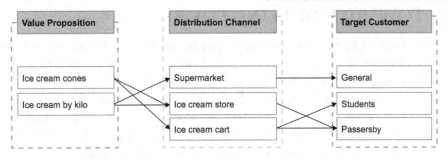

Figure 3.5: Value propositions, channels, and customer segments for Italian ice cream.

and the space where production is to be carried out. Capabilities define the key competences of a business. For an ice cream company, a secret recipe along with a group of people who can execute it might define a capability, another might be access to fresh fruit ingredients. Such capabilities might define the factors that distinguish our Italian company from its international counterparts. Finally, partnerships describe collaborations with external actors (such as other companies) through which our business produces and delivers its value propositions. A company that makes ice cream cones and a supermarket chain that carries only ice cream from our Italian company constitute examples of partnerships.

Finally, a business model is not complete without the concepts of revenue stream and cost. Revenue streams define the sources of income of a business. Note that revenue streams are not necessarily in one-to-one correspondence to value propositions. Google's most important value proposition is information, but its basic revenue comes from secondary value propositions, such as advertising.

The e^3value modeling framework [Gordijn and Akkermans, 2003] focuses on modeling value configurations in terms of networks of activities that create value. Each node of the network represents an actor/component who can create value and also needs value; each link represents a dependency between a consumer actor who has a need and a producer actor who can fulfill it. A path through the network represents a value chain with well-defined boundaries. Moreover, paths can take complex forms through AND/OR dependencies between one actor and multiple others.

The first modeling technique that tried to capture elements of a business model is the Resources-Events-Agents (REA) framework that McCarthy [1982] initially proposed as an accounting enterprise database model. REA is grounded on data modeling ideas from the '70s and adopts an entity-relationship (ER) modeling perspective. However, unlike the ER model, REA offers concepts that are better suited for accounting data, such as economic resources, the events that mark their consumption/production and the economic agents (including organizational units) who participate in such events.

3.5   TOWARD MODELING FOR BI

The three kinds of business modeling techniques reviewed so far are each relevant for BI in their own ways. However, they were not created with BI in mind. We now consider a recent proposal to address the specific needs of BI—the Business Intelligence Model.

Most BI systems to-date are based on models closely linked to the structure of available data. Even state-of-the-art systems that raise the abstraction level of BI systems require detailed knowledge of queries and data dimensions (e.g., IBM Cognos Express Reporter[1]). The gap between the world of business and the world of IT-supplied data remains one of the greatest barriers to the adoption of BI technologies [Stroh et al., 2011].

The *Business Intelligence Model (BIM)* [Barone et al., 2010a,b] is a business modeling language that offers concepts familiar to business decision makers such as goals, strategies, situations, influences, and indicators, so that business users can exploit the power of BI on their own terms. BIM draws upon the informal semantics of existing modeling techniques—including the Business Motivation Model (BMM) [Group, 2002], Strategy Maps (SM) [Kaplan and Norton, 2000], Balanced Scorecards (BSC) [Kaplan and Norton, 1992], and SWOT Analysis [Dealtry, 1994]—unifying them into a coherent schema, while providing formal semantics and support for reasoning.

Consider a consumer electronics retailer with vast amounts of data from diverse sources. Current BI tools require business analysts to work with reports and queries that are often data-oriented and difficult to modify. Instead, analysts would want to pose wide-ranging questions in business terms, such as:

- *Given the state of the business according to current data, if an economic slowdown is averted, will we be able to increase sales?*

In the remainder of this section, we highlight several key modeling constructs in BIM, and briefly outline the reasoning support provided by BIM. Figure 3.6 shows a sample BIM model for a consumer electronics retailer.

3.5.1   BIM CONCEPTS

Goal

A goal represents an objective in a business, e.g., "To increase sales." Goals may be (AND/OR) refined into sub-goals so that their satisfaction or achievement depends on that of their sub-goals. For example, "To increase sales" is AND-decomposed into sub-goals "To increase sales volume" and "To maintain gross margin." An OR-decomposition indicates that there is more than one way to achieve a goal. For example, "To open sales channels" and "To offer promotions" are alternative ways for achieving "To increase sales volume."

---

[1]http://www-142.ibm.com/software/products/ca/en/cognexprrepo/

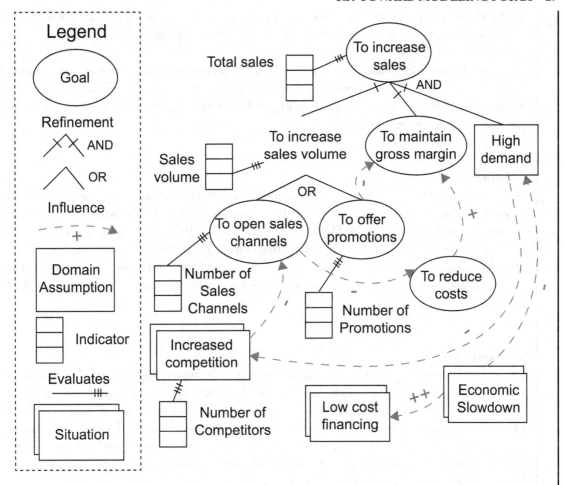

Figure 3.6: Example BIM schema model for a consumer electronics retailer.

Situation

Goal achievement is affected by internal and external factors. SWOT analysis (Strength, Weakness, Opportunity, and Threat) [Dealtry, 1994] can be used to help identify relevant factors. In BIM, these factors are captured using the notion of *situation*. While goals are actively sought by an organization, situations occur whether or not they are desired. A given situation may be favorable with respect to some organizational goals (positive influence links from situation to goal), while unfavorable to others (negative influence link). In our example, the "Increased competition" situation constitutes a threat to the "To open sales channels" goal, while "Economic slowdown" is a threat for "High

Demand" but an opportunity for "Low cost financing." Analogous to satisfaction levels for goals, a situation has an occurrence level which denotes the degree to which the situation occurs in the current state-of-affairs.

In addition to goals and situations, the BIM language supports the notion of processes within a business, as well as domain assumptions describing properties required for goal satisfaction. We see an example of a domain assumption in Figure 3.6 where "High demand" must be true in order for "Increase sales" to be satisfied.

Influence

Situations and goals can influence other situations and goals. The influence relationship in BIM is similar to the contribution relationship in several goal-oriented frameworks in requirements engineering [Chung et al., 2000, Dardenne et al., 1993, Yu, 1997]. One goal/situation influences another if its satisfaction/denial implies (partial) satisfaction/denial of the other. The influence strength is modeled using qualitative values: + (weak positive), ++ (strong positive), − (weak negative), and −− (strong negative). Quantitative probabilistic values can be used instead if available.

Indicator

Performance measures play an important role in helping businesses align their daily activities with their strategic objectives [Parmenter, 2007]. In BIM, an indicator is a metric that evaluates performance with respect to some objective, e.g., the degree of fulfillment for a strategic goal, or the quality of a business process or product. Each indicator is associated with a particular model element (e.g., goal, situation) through the *evaluates* relation. In Figure 3.6, the "Sales volume" indicator evaluates the "To increase sales volume" goal. Indicators constitute a conceptual bridge connecting a BIM model to business data found in a variety of data sources.

3.5.2   REASONING WITH BIM MODELS

Although the construction of a BIM model is useful as a means to clarify and communicate business objectives, strategies, and organizational situations, much of the benefits of BIM come from the capability to support reasoning thanks to its formal semantics. Reasoning with BIM allows an organization to answer strategic or monitoring questions such as the one posed earlier in this section. Here, we illustrate reasoning with indicators and qualitative reasoning from goal modeling techniques as applied to BIM.

In order to understand the meaning of current indicator values in business terms, comparable indicator *performance levels* can be propagated through a model. Each indicator has a *current value (cv)* which is evaluated against a set of parameters: *target (value)*, *threshold (value)*, and *worst (value)* [Parmenter, 2007]. The result of such an evaluation is a normalized value (ranging in

$[-1, 1] \subset \mathbb{R}$), which is often referred to as the *performance level* for an indicator. Example performance levels, making use of colored stoplights, are shown in Figure 3.7.

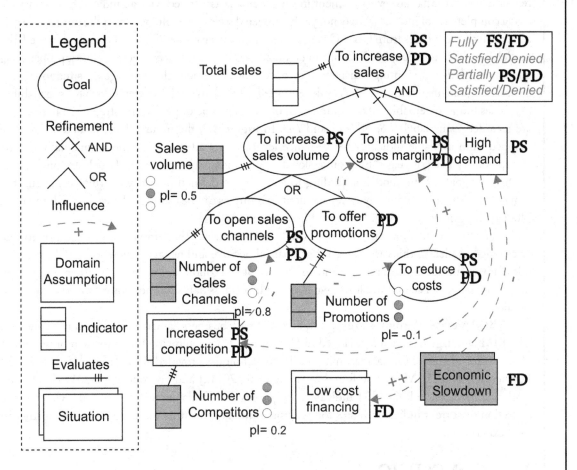

Figure 3.7: Example analysis results for the consumer electronics retailer schema.

Once performance levels have been produced for the required indicators, these values can be combined using business metrics, i.e., business specific formulae that describe how indicator values combine. Business metrics can combine current indicator values using explicit unit conversion factors (e.g., a new sales channel = $20,000 in sales). If unit conversion factors are not available, metrics could combine together available indicator performance levels as a way of estimating the performance of other indicators. For example, the indicators associated with the sub-goals "To open sales channels" and "To offer promotions" could be summed to produce a value for "Sales volume." Similarly, the negative influence of the situation "Increased competition" on "To open sales channels" could be expressed by subtracting the performance level of the former from the latter.

After each formula has been applied, results that lie outside the $[-1, 1]$ range must be normalized again. The results of our indicator propagation example are shown as part of Figure 3.7. The reader may notice that not every element in the schema is associated with an indicator. It is possible that a complete set of indicators may not yet have been developed or elicited from the domain. In this case, analysis techniques from Goal-Oriented Requirements Engineering can be applied to the BIM model, e.g., [Chung et al., 2000, Giorgini et al., 2004, Letier and Lamsweerde, 2004], propagating qualitative labels representing satisfaction or occurrence to model elements (goals, situations, processes, and domain assumptions). As Giorgini et al. [2004] argue, BIM elements have satisfiability (S) values but also deniability (D) values, each of which can be of partial (P) strength. These values are recorded using labels *FS, PS, PD,* and *FD*. In Figure 3.7, the input values, shaded in grey, are mapped from available indicator performance levels, or are added to the model manually as part of exploratory analysis (e.g., "Economic slowdown" is manually set to *FD*). Labels are propagated to the root goals of the model, according to a set of pre-defined propagation rules capturing the semantics of the relationships between elements. Examples can be found in the work of Chung et al. [2000], Giorgini et al. [2004], Letier and Lamsweerde [2004].

The final result shown in Figure 3.7 can be used to answer the sample analysis question for the electronics retailer. In this case, there is both partial positive and negative evidence for "To increase sales," given current indicator values and an absence of an economic slowdown. In other words, even in the case where an economic slowdown is averted, business data does not point toward an increase in sales.

BIM provides the means to explore and reason with business data in terms of business concepts. The BIM language has been formalized in Description Logic, allowing for a precise representation of semantics and use of formal reasoning similar to techniques provided above [Horkoff et al., 2012]. Further details on BIM may be found in [Jiang et al., 2011a] and [Barone et al., 2011a,b]. Future work will focus on linking BIM indicators to queries and available data sources, allowing for the collection of current indicator values for analysis. Linking indicators to data is discussed further in the next chapter.

3.6   CONCLUSIONS

Although BI technologies have seen rapid advances in recent years, these advances have not been complemented by corresponding developments in business modeling. The need for business level modeling is echoed in another lecture by Deutch and Milo [2012] in the same series, which addresses modeling and querying of business processes. Suitable business modeling languages and techniques are needed to enable business users to exploit the full potential of BI technologies. We expect more new business modeling approaches to emerge as BI continues to gain wider adoption.

CHAPTER 4

Vivification in BI

Patricia C. Arocena, Renée J. Miller, and John Mylopoulos

4.1 INTRODUCTION

BI offers tremendous potential for gaining insights into day-to-day business operations, as well as longer term opportunities and threats. The past decade has seen unprecedented interest in BI technologies and services, and a corresponding growth of the BI market. By now, most competitive organizations have a significant investment in BI, much of it technology-related, based on software tools and artefacts. But business people—be they executives, consultants, or analysts—are in general agreement that what helps them the most is not new gadgets producing a dizzying array of statistics. Instead, they need business data analyzed in their own terms, which are strategic objectives, business models and strategies, business processes, markets, trends, and risks. This gap between the world of business and the world of IT-supplied data remains today the greatest barrier to the adoption of BI technologies, as well as the greatest cost factor in their application to specific projects.

This gap is exacerbated by today's business world requirements for information-on-demand and agility that marginalizes many BI technologies. Information-on-demand is hampered when every business query requires its own data integration strategy, to be followed by evaluation of the query and interpretation of the results, to be done by technologists who will ultimately generate a response to the business query. Agility means that change is inevitable and ever-present in a business context, and must be factored into decision making processes as much as in everything else. Business objectives change, obstacles and opportunities are encountered and must be dealt with in a timely fashion.

To bridge the gap, we use a *business model* (also known as business schema) to represent business concepts, such as business entities and processes [Jiang et al., 2011b], and moreover, *schema mappings* from a database schema to a business model to specify *interpretations*. Data are then interpreted in terms of these concepts. For example, a hospital database may contain data about patient names, addresses, and health insurance numbers (hi#). Interpretation of these data means that some of them—e.g., name = 'John Smith,' address = '40 St. George Street,' hi# = 1234567—are ascribed to one patient. Likewise, the database may contain data about events, a hospital admission, an assignment to a ward, and a surgical operation. Interpretation, in this case, means that these events are associated with the entities that participated in them. Moreover, these events are grouped into aggregates that represent instances of processes, such as HospitalVisit that characterizes the day-to-day activities of a hospital. This form of interpretation has been called *vivification*, in the sense that it *brings data to life* (hence, vivifies), or *makes data more vivid* [Levesque, 1986].

Unfortunately (but unsurprisingly!), the vivification of data in terms of business model concepts is not a simple one-to-one mapping. Much like the task of finding who visited a crime scene on the basis of footprints, there are in general many possible mappings from data to business entities and processes. For instance, the hospital database may mention N times patients named 'John Smith.' These may correspond to 1, 2, ... or N different patients. Likewise, a surgical operation may be part of one patient's hospital visit or another's, depending on the data associated with the operation, and how these data have been interpreted.

Our aim in this chapter is to introduce the reader to the problem of vivification in the context of BI and to examine a number of important research contributions in the literature, bringing together previously disparate bodies of work and suggesting some future directions. Specifically, we use schema mappings from a database schema to a business model to specify interpretations. We view the vivification task as one of removing *incompleteness* or *uncertainty* from this mapping. An important aspect of our treatment is making vivification systematic so that the choices made in interpreting data through a business schema can be documented and analyzed along with the data. Indeed, a primary motivation for our work is the desire to document the myriad of choices that necessarily need to be made when using data to get the answers business users need. It is important that these choices not be *ad hoc*. Rather, they should be made based on available evidence. The choices and the context in which they are made should be documented so they can be revisited if the available evidence changes.

The rest of the chapter is organized as follows. In Section 4.2, we present a motivating example illustrating a business schema and an IT-supplied database (or data warehouse) schema and some of the ways in which they may differ. In Section 4.3, we discuss the vivification problem as it has been defined and studied in the literature. In Section 4.4, we consider how vivification can be used in BI and present elements of a formal framework to bring IT-supplied data to life in terms of business concepts. In Sections 4.5 and 4.6, we review current and future strategies for doing BI vivification. In Section 4.7, we briefly discuss some directions for future research. Last, we conclude in Section 4.8.

4.2   A MOTIVATING EXAMPLE

We begin by presenting an example of a business schema and an IT-supplied database schema, with special emphasis on the mappings that can be leveraged to provide data-to-business interpretations.

Business Schema

Consider a business schema describing how a hospital operates as a business organization and how it handles business content. We present parts of an example business schema in the top portion of Figure 4.1. The business schema identifies some *business entity types* of interest: patients (`Patient`), physicians (`Doctor`), locations (`Location`), and documents (`Document`). There are two types of patients, outpatients (`OutPatient`) and inpatients (`InPatient`). Likewise, there are different types of

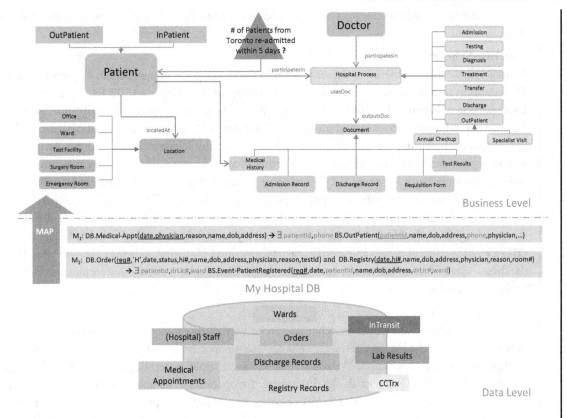

Figure 4.1: An illustration of a hospital business mapping scenario.

locations and documents. Besides entity types, the business schema includes a number of hospital services (`Hospital Process`) to diagnose and treat patients, each of which is specified using a *business process model* (not shown in the illustration). Our examples will make use of the Admission Business Process (`Admission`) which is in charge of handling hospital admissions. The `Admission` process model formally describes the participants of the process, such as a person seeking hospitalization—in his or her role as 'New Patient'—and a physician authorizing the hospitalization—in his or her role as 'Admitting Doctor'; a collection of *activities* or tasks that must be performed within the execution of the process, such as activity 'Register a Patient'; a collection of *business events* that mark the occurrence of activities (e.g., the start, end, or any other relevant milestone within an activity) and which are directly observable in the data, such as the arrival of a patient by ambulance (`Event-PatientArriving`); and last, a specific desired outcome, such as the creation of a new admission record (`Admission Record`). Our techniques are agnostic to the specific formalisms used for describing business entity types and process models. In our examples, we will assume that the process model describes inputs and outputs for each activity or event type along with optional pre-conditions and post-conditions (as this type of information is commonly specified in process models).

Database Schema

In addition, we assume there is a database schema that models the data collected by the operational IT systems in the organization. For our example, we use the My Hospital DB schema shown in the lower portion of Figure 4.1. Table Staff records information about health care practitioners working for the hospital, such as doctors and nurses. Table Medical-Appt stores details of outpatient clinic appointments, including the date of the appointment, the physician of choice, and details about the requesting patient. Tables Registry and InTransit store hospital admission records and transfer requests by ambulance, respectively. Information about wards is described in Table Ward. Table Order records information about requisitions, including the type ('H' for hospitalization and 'L' for laboratory), date and status, information about the patient, and a laboratory test identifier (e.g., Immunology-Rubella-24), if applicable. All laboratory test results are stored in Table Result. Table CCTrx records relevant details about credit card transactions. Note that, as is the case with operational databases, some of these tables may be recording information about events that implement different business processes.

Business Mappings

The business schema and database schemas can be very different as they are often developed and evolve independently. We use *business mapping rules* to specify the relationship between concepts in these two disparate schemas. We use source-to-target tuple-generating dependencies (s-t tgds) to express these rules [Fagin et al., 2005a], where the operational database provides the *source* data that is used to populate the *target* business concepts. Business mapping rule M_1 states that for each outpatient medical appointment record, there must be an associated OutPatient business entity, whose name, date of birth, address, and physician values are the same as those of the medical appointment record. This constraint is encoded by using the same participating variable names on both sides of the implication ($\rightarrow$ symbol). We underline variables names that serve as key identifiers; we refer to the left-hand-side expression as the *source* expression, and the right-hand-side as the *target* expression. Notice that the target expression in rule M_1 fails to specify what values should be given for the patient hospital identifier and phone attributes of an OutPatient, as shown by the use of existentially quantified variables patientId and phone, respectively. Similarly, business mapping rule M_2 asserts that an association between hospitalization requisition orders and patient registry entries based on foreign keys signals the occurrence of a particular event type in the data, and therefore this must be accounted for in the target. The source expression indicates this association by joining tables Order and Registry on some common attributes such as *hi#, date, name*, and *dob*. The target expression accordingly mirrors the occurrence of a pre-admission registration in the business by stating the existence of a business event (Event-PatientRegistered). As before, some values in the target expression are left underspecified.

Business Queries

As business analysts evaluate and make strategic decisions, they usually pose queries against the business schema instance.[1] In the context of a hospital organization, for example, typical queries may ask "What is the average length of stay of patients who have suffered a hip fracture and are over 65 years-old?," "Are the Emergency Room wait times within the provincial target?," and among many others, "How many patients from Toronto have been re-admitted within 5 business days?." These business queries, as is common in BI, require aggregation, grouping, and trending across various business concepts over a given period of time.

Note how the presence of incompleteness (and uncertainty) in business mapping rules sheds light on the various ways in which our motivating business and database schemas differ. Even though the database contains information about patients and activities involving patients, the concept of patient as a business entity does not exist in the database. Thus, the mapping does not tell us how to uniquely identify patients from the source data. The database may also not have complete information about the execution of business processes. Furthermore, it may be hard to correlate the various events recorded in the database to understand which correspond to a single instance of a business process. A single hospital requisition and a one-time patient registration record, for example, may result in *many* hospital admissions, as is usually the case with inpatients undergoing recurrent therapeutic procedures. The importance of creating an interpretation of the data consistent with the business becomes apparent at query time, as we discuss next.

4.3   THE VIVIFICATION PROBLEM

A business schema is most useful if it is instantiated with complete and accurate information. This information is naturally derived from the IT-supplied databases (or warehouses), but since these databases are often designed for a different purpose (supporting operational systems), it is rare that they provide complete and consistent business data. Hence, BI practitioners must deal with missing and uncertain information on a daily basis. Querying and reasoning over incomplete information is complex and computationally intractable [Imielinski and Lipski, 1983]. Furthermore, it may be unacceptable, from a business stand point, to answer "I don't know" when a user asks for the number of patients. In this section, we review two *foundational techniques* for interpreting data.

4.3.1   KNOWLEDGE BASE VIVIFICATION

Consider a knowledge base (KB) as a finite collection of facts about the world of interest. We say a KB is *incomplete* when it asserts that one of many facts is true, but without being able to individually determine the truth of each individual fact. Continuing with our motivating example, a KB indicating that 'John Smith' is a recently admitted inpatient in either the Cardiology Ward or the Maternity Unit, without saying which of the two locations is correct, is considered incomplete. Incompleteness in this example arises due to a disjunction in the representation of the facts. In general, as we exemplify next, incompleteness may be attributable to a number of logical constructs, such as disjunction, existential quantification, and negation [Levesque, 1986].

---

[1]We use the term (database or business) instance to refer to the population of a schema.

Sources of Incompleteness in a KB	
Disjunctions	$AssignedTo('John\ Smith', Cardiology) \lor AssignedTo('John\ Smith', Maternity)$ We still do not know John Smith's exact ward location.
Existentials	$\exists\ patientId\ InPatient(patientId, 'John\ Smith', \ldots)$ John Smith has an *unknown* patient hospital identifier.
Negations	$\neg\ HeadPhysician(Cardiology, 'Dr.Quaid')$ We still do not know who is the head physician of Cardiology.

To act in the face of incompleteness, Levesque [1986] proposed a technique called *Vivification* for transforming an incomplete KB into a complete representation, where reasoning can be simply reduced to standard database querying. Vivifying a KB amounts to eliminating any sources of incompleteness that may appear in its representational form, and most importantly, placing symbols in the KB into a *one-to-one correspondence* to objects of interest in the world and their relationships. For example, confronted with the disjunctive fact that 'John Smith' is either located in the Cardiology Ward or in the Maternity Unit, we might be able to resolve this issue by looking up the location of the admitting physician's office. In doing so, we use the relationship between admitted inpatients and admitting doctors in the business to establish proper connections among the data.

The following property, adapted from Levesque [1986] to our BI interpretation problem, offers a tool for characterizing the type of business schema instantiation we attempt to derive.

Definition 4.1 Vividness Property A complete business schema instance satisfies a property called *vividness* if the following two conditions hold:

1. **Entity Correspondence.** There is a one-to-one correspondence between groups of database records in the database and business entities of interest in the business schema.

2. **Relationship Correspondence.** For every relevant relationship in the business schema, there is a connection among database records in the database such that the relationship holds among a group of business concepts in the business if and only if the appropriate connection exists among the corresponding database records in the data world.

The notion of vividness is relevant to the task of interpreting the world of IT-supplied data in terms of the world of business. First, it corresponds well to the common *ad hoc* practice of 'filling in the blanks' to coerce data into a form that is complete and adequate for business querying. Second, various types of business data, such as business plans, strategies, and goals, are already conveyed using vivid or visual descriptions. This is, ultimately, the type of data business analysts have in their mind when issuing queries. In this chapter, we argue that vivification provides a principled foundation for doing the data-to-business interpretation.

4.3.2 DATA EXCHANGE

Vivification is also important in translating between two databases [Popa et al., 2002]. Schema mappings (first-order logic expressions) are used to express the relationship between two database schemas. Given a schema mapping, the problem of data exchange was introduced by Fagin et al. [2005a], and defined as the problem of translating data structured under a source schema into an instance of a target schema that reflects the source data as accurately as possible. An important aspect of this work was the recognition that even in exchanging data between two IT database schemas, it is rare that a complete target instance (database) can be created. The notion of a *universal solution* was introduced as the best solution for representing data as accurately as possible, but these instances are often incomplete. In BI, we could build on this foundation to provide a way to systematically refine schema mappings to remove uncertainty so that the universal solution of the refined (vivified) mapping is a complete database. As an illustration, we use an example which is originally due to Arocena et al. [2012].

Example 4.2   Consider a simple schema mapping stating how to populate a target insurance database from a source inpatient registry table using s-t tgds:

$$\text{Registry}\,(name, dob, addr) \rightarrow \exists\,\textbf{policyId}\,\text{Insurance}\,(\textbf{policyId}, name, dob)$$

This mapping indicates that for each inpatient registry tuple, there must be an associated insurance record in the target, whose name and date of birth values are the same as those of the inpatient registry. The variables *name, dob, addr* are universally quantified. Notice that the target expression (right-hand-side of the implication) uses an existential variable `policyId` to indicate that the policy number is underspecified. Figure 4.2 shows a source instance I and a universal solution (target instance) J with labeled NULL values (i.e., N_1, N_2, and N_3) instead of concrete policy numbers.

Source Instance I				Target Instance J		
Name	DOB	Address		PolicyId	Name	DOB
Marge Wood	05-05-1927	Markham		N_1	Marge Wood	05-05-1927
Marge Wood	05-05-1927	London		N_2	Marge Wood	05-05-1927
Margret Wood	05-05-1925	London		N_3	Margret Wood	05-05-1925

Figure 4.2: A data exchange scenario: source instance and universal solution.

Schema mappings record the decisions made in translating data. Data exchange permits the precise modeling of the uncertainty in a translation. In the above target instance, the use of three labeled NULLs indicates that the three tuples could refer to three different people, or to just two people (perhaps Marge moved so the first two NULLs should share a single value) or to a single person (perhaps there were inconsistencies in entering information and all three tuples refer to one person). If a business needs to track the number of patients, someone must make a choice on how to resolve this uncertainty.

When computing universal solutions, semi-automated schema mapping systems, such as Clio [Fagin et al., 2009] and ++Spicy [Marnette et al., 2011], simulate the presence of labeled NULL values using Skolem functions. Traditionally, *Skolem functions* have been used to generate entity (or object) identifiers such as $f(x_1)$, $f(x_2)$, ... where $x_1, x_2, ...$ are existing attributes or identifiers [Abiteboul et al., 1999]. The premise for choosing Skolem terms is that they should produce object identifiers that are unique enough, but not too unique as to fail in establishing the proper grouping or desired semantics [Hull and Yoshikawa, 1990, Papakonstantinou et al., 1996, Popa et al., 2002]. Clio's data exchange system, in particular, systematically relies on using (one-to-one) Skolem functions for generating labeled NULL values based on a set of source values.[2] These Skolems serve as generic *vivid* values.

Example 4.3 In our previous example, by replacing the existential variable policyId with Skolem $f(name, dob, addr)$, we can then use 'f(Marge Wood, 05-05-1927, Markham)', 'f(Marge Wood, 05-05-1927, London)', and 'f(Margret Wood, 05-05-1925, London)' as different but unique identifiers in instance J. By using distinct values, we are modeling the interpretation that there are three distinct patients.

Next, we present a first step toward a unifying framework for studying vivification in BI. We build on the foundation of data exchange to view the vivification task as one of removing incompleteness or uncertainty from a schema mapping. We advocate a declarative approach where vivification decisions are documented in a formalism that supports automated reasoning (in the same way schema mappings permit formal reasoning about a translation) and in which we can define precisely when an interpretation (or set of vivification decisions) is vivid.

4.4 FORMAL FRAMEWORK

We now present elements of a formal framework for interpreting data in BI, using the concepts of database schema, business schema, business mapping, vivification assumptions, and business queries.

In a BI setting, we have a source database schema DB and a target business schema BS, which are disparate and may have been independently developed. As illustrated in our motivating example, the **source database schema** comprises a number of relations $R_1, R_2, ..., R_n$, some of which may be recording information about the instrumentation of business processes. Our proposal is general enough to accommodate not only mainstream relational databases but also specific technologies such as data warehouses. The **target business schema**, on the other side, offers a conceptual model of a particular organization in terms of business concepts $T_1, T_2, ..., T_m$, such as business entities, business processes, and business events. This description may be given in some business modeling formalism [Jiang et al., 2011b]. In addition, we have a set $\mathcal{M}$ of **business mapping rules** describing the relationship between the source and target schemas. The mapping language we use for illustration

---

[2]In practice, Skolem functions may be encoded using strings that concatenate the Skolem function's name with the string representing its arguments.

is based on the widely used database concept of s-t tgds [Fagin et al., 2005a]. Each mapping rule may indicate a correspondence between a query over the source database ϕ_{DB} and a query over the target ψ_{BS} involving either business entities or business events. Formally, each mapping rule is of the form:

$$\forall \mathbf{z}, \mathbf{x}(\phi_{DB}(\mathbf{z}, \mathbf{x}) \rightarrow \exists \mathbf{y} \psi_{BS}(\mathbf{x}, \mathbf{y})), \tag{4.1}$$

where $\phi_{DB}(\mathbf{z}, \mathbf{x})$ is a query over the source database schema and $\psi_{BS}(\mathbf{x}, \mathbf{y})$ is a query over the target business schema. Intuitively, $\mathbf{x}$ represents the information that is exchanged from the source into the target, and $\mathbf{y}$ represent the information that is unknown in the target. We also use a set $\mathcal{A}$ of **vivification assumptions** to characterize desired properties or constraints over any instantiation of the target business schema. These may be given using any constraint language, such as tuple-generating dependencies (tgds) and equality-generating dependencies (egds) [Abiteboul et al., 1995]. In addition to having functional dependencies and cardinality constraints, we may also have assumptions that state a particular choice among a set of possible facts to resolve incompleteness or inconsistency. Last, we have a set $\mathcal{Q}$ of **business queries** in some query language formalism. We assume a traditional query answering semantics over complete databases which will determine, for a given query, what parts of a given business schema instance must be complete to compute a certain query answer. For example, if we consider Example 4.2, using this mapping alone, we would not be able to answer a query that counts the number of insurance policies. This mapping leaves the insurance policy identifiers incomplete, and therefore leaves incomplete the decision on whether two policies are the same. However, a query that asks if Marge Wood is a patient can be answered with certainty. We can use certain query answering semantics [Abiteboul et al., 1991] to reason about whether an instance of a business schema is sufficient to answer with certainty a given set of queries.

Definition 4.4 A BI setting (DB, BS, $\mathcal{M}, \mathcal{A}, \mathcal{Q}$) consists of a database schema DB, a business schema BS, a set $\mathcal{M}$ of business mapping rules, a set $\mathcal{A}$ of vivification assumptions, and a set $\mathcal{Q}$ of business queries. Let I be a source instance over DB and J a target instance over BS such that $\langle I, J \rangle$ satisfy $\mathcal{M}$ and $\mathcal{A}$.

- We say that J is *vivid* if any tuple in J is null-free and all constants in J are justified by either I (the source instance at hand) or by $\mathcal{A}$.

- We say that J is *vivid for a set of queries* $\mathcal{Q}$ if for every query $q \in \mathcal{Q}$, the sets of possible and certain answers for $q(J)$ coincide.

It follows from this definition that a vivid business schema instance needs to be *discovered*. This needs to be done in the light of concepts in the business schema, any given vivification assumptions, and a set of business queries of interest. We advocate an approach in which the vivification decisions are documented by modifying the mapping and assumptions so that they produce a vivid instance (or one that is vivid for the set of relevant business queries).

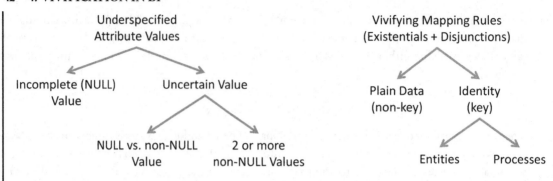

Figure 4.3: The scope of vivification in business mapping rules.

From Data to Business Entities and Processes

Our vivification process starts by considering an initial set $\mathcal{M}$ of business mapping rules between a database schema and a business schema, and a *universal solution* [Fagin et al., 2005a] that this mapping entails. More specifically, we turn our attention to how we can coax *incompleteness* and *uncertainty* out of $\mathcal{M}$ and $\mathcal{A}$. This involves systematically choosing and applying vivification strategies over existentials and disjunctions (and negations depending on the mapping language) to elicit an interpretation of the source data that is consistent with the business assumptions and queries. As we discuss in Section 4.6, these strategies include finding mapping tables or finding default values from the business context to resolve existential variables, and using business rules to resolve inconsistencies and/or favor relevant disjuncts.

Vivification Scope

As we illustrate in Figure 4.3, *incompleteness* may arise when a mapping rule fails to specify what value should be given to a target attribute or when the source database I fails to provide a value, thus rendering an incomplete NULL value during mapping execution. Conversely, *uncertainty* may arise due to having more than one way of populating a given target value (for example, at least one mapping rule includes an existential or disjunction of values over the attribute in question) or due to a database that does not enforce business-level requirements (for example, a business rule saying every patient must provide a single health insurance policy number and the database provides multiple numbers). In general, we distinguish between vivifying non-key and key attribute positions in mapping rules. We refer to these as *data vivification* and *identity vivification*, respectively. The first is concerned with supplying one or more certain data values to a target business concept. The second one attempts to bring operational data to life in terms of business entities and processes by correctly associating data with specific instances of real-world business concepts. In the next sections, we discuss a number of current and future vivification strategies for vivifying business concepts.

4.5   CURRENT VIVIFICATION STRATEGIES

Incompleteness and uncertainty play prominent roles in information integration. Many techniques have been proposed to minimize the incidence of incompleteness and uncertainty in the context of database-to-database schema mappings. The vast majority of these techniques are not specifically tailored to BI, but are nonetheless relevant for doing the data-to-business interpretation. Here we briefly discuss a few by considering their intent viewed from our vivification perspective.

4.5.1   STRATEGIES FOR DEALING WITH INCOMPLETENESS

Certain Answers

In the context of data exchange and integration, the widely adopted query answering semantics is that of certain answers in incomplete databases [Abiteboul et al., 1991, Imielinski and Lipski, 1983]. Intuitively, we say the *certain answers* of a query q is the set of all tuples t that appear in every possible solution J, regardless of which particular solution we have chosen to materialize. Universal solutions [Fagin et al., 2005a] have the unique property that the certain answers to unions of conjunctive queries can be obtained by evaluating the query on any universal solution, and importantly universal solutions are the only solutions possessing this property. Afrati and Kolaitis [2008] tailored this semantics for answering aggregate queries in data exchange. A major drawback of certain answers is perhaps the fact that their computation for non-positive queries relies on logical entailment, and cannot be computed using standard relational queries [Franconi et al., 2012]. This furthers our motivation for vivifying incomplete target instances.

Minimizing Data Exchange Solutions

Of all possible data exchange solutions we could materialize, universal solutions appear as the most general possible solutions, offering no more and no less than what is strictly required for data exchange. Fagin et al. [2005a] describe an algorithm based on the chase procedure for computing a *canonical* universal solution. In a follow-up proposal, they show how the size of universal solutions (where by size we mean the number of tuples) can be further minimized and introduce the notion of *core solution* [Fagin et al., 2005b]. Core solutions are the most compact universal solutions we can possibly materialize. Recently, specialized algorithms for efficiently computing core solutions using SQL queries haven been proposed [Marnette et al., 2010, Mecca et al., 2009, ten Cate et al., 2009]. Core solutions may still be incomplete and thus may not be sufficient for supporting some business queries.

Normalizing Schema Mappings

Many different mapping formalisms have been proposed in recent years, some of which allow the expression of correlation semantics as well as grouping and data merging [Alexe et al., 2010, Fuxman et al., 2006]. Mapping specifications using these formalisms often yield more compact target instances with less redundancy and fewer labeled NULL values. With this end in mind, Gottlob et al. introduce a system of rewrite rules to minimize any set of s-t tgds into an equivalent optimal one, resulting in the first notion of a *normal form* for schema mappings [Gottlob et al., 2011]. This simplification theory empowers many existing applications dependant on the concrete syntactic representation of tgds.

Refining Schema Mappings through Data Examples

In many situations, mapping designers may need to understand the semantics of schema mappings from their syntactic specifications. This occurs, for example, when semi-automatic mapping tools suggest multiple differing schema mappings [Alexe et al., 2008b], or when the schemas and/or mappings evolve [Velegrakis et al., 2003, Yu and Popa, 2005]. A line of research has focused on providing some relief to this problem by illustrating and explaining the behavior of schema mappings using *data examples* [Alexe et al., 2011b, Chiticariu and Tan, 2006, Yan et al., 2001]. Data examples have also been used to aid mapping designers in refining and deriving schema mappings [Alexe et al., 2008a, 2011c,a, Fletcher and Wyss, 2009, Gottlob and Senellart, 2010]. Behind all this body of work lies the true intent of enriching schema mappings with semantics and removing uncertainty, which is also the underlying goal of vivifying business mappings.

Imputation of Missing Values

The literature abounds in studies of methods for imputing missing data values, including but not limited to statistical and probabilistic analyses. While an overview of data imputation lies outside the scope of this present work, we wish to cite the work of de S. Ribeiro et al. [2011]. The authors discuss the problem of imputing missing data values in the context of Extract-Transform-Load (ETL)[3] transformations by relying on data provenance. As is the case with most data imputation methods [Raghunathan, 2004], the proposed strategy makes certain *assumptions* about why fact attribute values are missing and exploits them to suggest plausible non-NULL values. In contrast, we are advocating an approach in which such assumptions are made explicit in the BI setting to record and permit reasoning about these assumptions (as they may change over time).

4.5.2   STRATEGIES FOR DEALING WITH UNCERTAINTY

Consistent Answers

In some data management scenarios, uncertainty may arise due to *inconsistency*. This usually occurs when integrating data from disparate sources or when it is necessary to enforce a set of *integrity constraints* in a target schema. Informally, we say a database instance is inconsistent if it violates one or more target constraints. An alternative approach to cleaning the inconsistent database is dealing with potential inconsistencies of the data at query time, and retrieving only those answers that are consistent in all virtual *database repairs*. Consistent query answering was initially proposed by Arenas et al. [1999] and has been explored from many different angles, including that of efficient query rewriting in the context of key dependencies [Fuxman et al., 2005, Fuxman and Miller, 2007] and the computation of preferred consistent answers [Staworko et al., 2012]. The use of *consistent answers* (like certain answers) is a viable approach for computing a (conservative) set of vivid answers.

---

[3]ETL is the process by which data from multiple sources is consolidated into a data warehouse.

Duplicate Detection

The problem of duplicate detection (a.k.a., entity identification, data deduplication, or record linkage) resides in identifying multiple records (scattered among several data sources) that potentially refer to the same real-world entity. Deduplication techniques aim primarily at solving identity conflicts in the data. Numerous approaches have been proposed for vivifying real-world entities [Elmagarmid et al., 2007] and most of them are applicable in our framework. Some approaches rely on semantic similarity rules to match records [Benjelloun et al., 2009, Galhardas et al., 2001, Hernández and Stolfo, 1998]. These declarative approaches facilitate encapsulating domain-specific knowledge in matching rules. Moreover, these rules can be easily documented and communicated within teams of business users, and importantly changed as business requirements change.

Data Fusion

Data fusion is the process of fusing multiple records representing the same real-world entity into a single, consistent, and concise representation [Bleiholder and Naumann, 2008]. This process is also known as data consolidation or entity resolution in the literature. In fusing data from different sources, we analyze two kinds of attribute-level data conflicts, missing attribute values and uncertainties due to the presence of contradicting values. Bleiholder and Naumann [2005] propose a relational extension of SQL, known as FUSE BY operator, which allows a user to declaratively specify fusion strategies to resolve attribute-level discrepancies. Unlike other advanced relational operators proposed in the context of data integration (minimum union [Galindo-Legaria, 1994], match join [Yan and Özsu, 1999], and merge [Greco et al., 2001]), FUSE BY is able to handle uncertainties due to contradicting values. Like approaches based on outer union, FUSE BY may introduce additional NULL values due to union compatibility issues among data sources. Most of these fusion techniques are still applicable in our proposed framework. An important difference is the point of intervention at which the techniques are applied. In particular, we view mapping rules as crucial tools for declaratively recording and reasoning about resolution and fusion decisions. Notably, while duplicate detection and data fusion are mostly viewed as one-time-only offline tasks, we envision a process where vivification strategies can be iteratively applied, assessed, and revised as real-time information becomes available or changes.

4.5.3 SUMMARY OF OTHER RELEVANT WORK

Close in spirit to the BI vivification perspective presented in this chapter is the work of Sismanis et al. [2009]. This work proposes a resolution-aware query answering model for OLAP applications, where uncertainty about business entities is handled dynamically at query time; the work, however, does not discuss how to deal with incomplete or uncertain attribute values in a general BI context. Among recently studied information quality criteria, Naumann's completeness of data measures the amount of non-NULL values in a database instance (this is done in comparison to a potentially complete universal relation) [Naumann, 2002]. This criterion embodies a model that can also be used to calculate the completeness of query answers which result from combining sources through merge operators; as such, this work can be leveraged in our framework to encode specific completeness assumptions or constraints over business interpretations. Our perspective also relates to both data exchange and semantic web efforts on bridging open and closed world reasoning [Libkin, 2006, Sengupta et al., 2011]. Moreover, our perspective complements the work of van der Aalst [2011] in Business Process Modeling (BPM). While their emphasis is on discovering and enhancing business process models from event logs in the data, ours is on providing an interpretation from observed events with respect to business models.

4.6   TOWARD ADAPTIVE VIVIFICATION STRATEGIES

None of the previously discussed techniques appears to foster an *adaptive* mind-set toward removing incompleteness and uncertainty in business mapping rules. Indeed, many of them are being deployed with very little business perspective in mind, usually as one-time-only processes over the IT-supplied data. The choices made to interpret data are thus heavily influenced by the desire to cover as much ground as possible without further thought or reflection on what is sufficient for decision making.

In our framework, we advocate a shift in focus from *one-size-fits-all* interpretations of the data to *vivid* ones, which are solely discovered in the light of documented assumptions and business requirements. Toward that end, we outline three high-level strategies for vivifying business mapping rules: *acceptance*, *default*, and *resolution*. By applying these over any mapping rule, we obtain a space of alternatives yielding different interpretations of the data in terms of business concepts. Figure 4.4 depicts our classification of vivification strategies.[4] Next, we examine the semantics associated with each high-level strategy and, alongside, we present some examples.

4.6.1   VIVIFICATION BY ACCEPTANCE

Vivification by acceptance describes a strategy (`IGNORE`) that accepts the existence of incomplete or uncertain attributes in the mapping and, moreover, makes no decision with respect to how existential variables could be filled in or resolved to support effective query answering. Most of the strategies discussed in Section 4.5 follow this neutral scheme. By choosing to pass incomplete and uncertain values to the user or application (i.e., ignoring `NULL` values), the system relinquishes control over the expected quality of the target business instance (and also of any queries posed over it). This strategy appears to be most useful when the context surrounding the vivification task imposes no requirements on vivified attributes.

Example 4.5   Consider business mapping rule M_1 from Figure 4.1 and the task of vivifying a non-key attribute position over a business entity concept:

> `DB.Medical-Appt` (*date, physician, reason, name, dob, address*) $\rightarrow \exists$ *patientId*, **phone**
> `BS.OutPatient` (*patientId, name, dob, address*, **phone**, *physician*, . . .)

---

[4]This classification has been inspired by Bleiholder and Naumann's data fusion taxonomy [Bleiholder and Naumann, 2006].

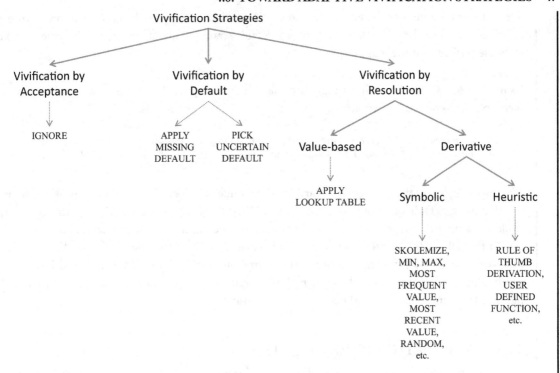

Figure 4.4: A classification of adaptive vivification strategies.

As can be seen in this mapping rule, there is incompleteness with respect to phone numbers (in bold face). That is, the rule fails to specify which value or values should be given for the phone attribute when populating an Outpatient business entity. Choosing to IGNORE this source of incompleteness means that any materialized target instance will have NULL values over the phone attribute, a decision that may still be adequate if phone numbers are irrelevant in the context of decision making.

4.6.2   VIVIFICATION BY DEFAULT

Vivification by default strategies deal with incompleteness and uncertainty by applying a default decision. Two possible default strategies are APPLY MISSING VALUE DEFAULT and PICK UNCERTAIN DEFAULT. When employing the first default strategy, we acknowledge the existence of an incomplete attribute and replace the corresponding existential variable in the mapping with either a single *default data value* (constant) or a disjunction of values. In selecting default values, we may leverage user input or domain knowledge derived from the business schema. The second default strategy acts on uncertain attributes (i.e., those exhibiting both NULL and non-NULL data values) by intuitively discarding any NULL values and then, picking one of their non-NULL data values. To do this, we refine the mapping to replace an existential variable with a chosen source attribute according to other relevant mapping rules or the business context. Notice that this approach succeeds in preserving an existing data value. In general, vivification by default strategies are amenable to vivifying non-key attribute positions in the mapping.

Example 4.6   Consider business mapping rule M_2 from Figure 4.1 and how we could vivify any incompleteness over the **ward** attribute of recently registered inpatients.

> DB.Order $(req\#, H, date, status, hi\#, name, \dots)$ $\land$ DB.Registry $(date, hi\#, name, \dots, room\#)$
> $\rightarrow \exists\, patientId, drLic\#, \textbf{ward}$ BS.Event-PatientRegistered $(req\#, date, patientId, \dots, \textbf{ward})$

This mapping leaves the values of the **ward** attribute underspecified. A plausible vivification strategy is enforcing a default value over this attribute (APPLY MISSING VALUE DEFAULT strategy). This could certainly be done if in our motivating business schema, there were a hospital business policy stating that all newly admitted inpatients should be assigned to the hospital's Triage Ward (a choice followed by most hospital organizations during viral outbreaks). By making explicit this business-specific knowledge, we enable decision making based on indicators or queries that, for example, monitor the number of occupied beds per hospital ward.

4.6.3   VIVIFICATION BY RESOLUTION

In contrast to previous strategies, vivification by resolution strategies aim at considering the mapping and any available domain knowledge before deciding how to resolve incompleteness or uncertainty. Two main classes of resolution strategies are *value-based* and *derivative* strategies. Value-based strategies resolve incompleteness or uncertainty by using look-up or mapping tables (APPLY LOOKUP TABLE), i.e., they rely on explicit encodings of resolved values. The assumption is that these tables may be available (though perhaps missed by a manual or automated mapping process). Furthermore, the user may have expertise on how to use them to supply missing values or on how to correct uncertain ones. Derivative strategies attempt to compute a resolved value by considering existing values and any insightful information given by the context in which the vivification task is being done. We distinguish between *symbolic* and *heuristic* resolution strategies. Symbolic strategies compute a representative value from existing data and use this value to resolve any incompleteness or uncertainty. SKOLEMIZE relies on Skolem functions to generate unique identifiers or values from existing attribute values; by customizing the construction of Skolem terms, the technique may successfully be used to resolve or disambiguate both key and non-key attribute positions in the mapping. In Example 4.3, if we change the arguments to the Skolem function to be just *dob*, then we are stating that there are two (not three) patients (i.e., the first two tuples from Figure 4.2 represent the same person). Other symbolic strategies employ standard aggregation and statistical resolution functions (e.g., MIN, MAX, MOST FREQUENT VALUE, etc.). In cases where timestamp information is part of the source schema, recency strategies such as MOST RECENT VALUE may be used to resolve incomplete or uncertain values. Last, heuristic resolution strategies strive to vivify incompleteness or uncertainty by using domain or application specific RULE OF THUMB DERIVATION strategies, which may be user-defined or system derived.

Example 4.7   Continuing with Example 4.5, consider how two different resolution strategies, APPLY LOOKUP TABLE and SKOLEMIZE, can be used in tandem to vivify incomplete phone numbers. Assume we have a data mapping table which relates phone numbers to either patient names or addresses. With this at hand, we may attempt rewriting mapping rule M_1 to bring out known phone numbers from associations between DB.Medical-Appt and the newly introduced mapping table. To support lossy cases, we need to add a fallback mapping rule that generates, for example, Skolem terms from existing patient names (e.g., $f('John Smith')$) instead of NULL phone values. In conjunction, the two refined mapping rules guarantee that any population of the Outpatient business entity-type has non-NULL phone values.

Example 4.8   Assume that the Admission Business Process (Admission) specification (presented in Section 4.2) requires that a hospital admission (Admission Record) indicates the name of a consulting physician, in addition to recording the name of the admitting physician and some other attributes. We may have a business mapping rule that is able to populate some information about admission registrations, but the mapping rule leaves underspecified the value for the consultant attribute. In principle, any query counting admissions based on the number of consulting physicians cannot be answered. Suppose there is a hospital business policy indicating that in case of incompleteness, the consulting physician is the head of the department of the patient's ward. This piece of domain knowledge lets us not only fill in the blanks (RULE OF THUMB DERIVATION strategy), but also tells us that there is only one missing attribute value per admission record.

4.7   DIRECTIONS FOR FUTURE RESEARCH

Throughout the discussion in this chapter we emphasize the importance of vivifying data according to the requirements of the business, in a rigorous and systematic matter. Guided by Frege's *context principle* to "never ask for the meaning of a word in isolation, but only in the context of a proposition" [Frege, 1980], our formal framework aims at interpreting incomplete or uncertain attribute values in the proper scope of data to business translation. The notion of context is central to vivification; we suggest looking to the business schema, the business process model, and, importantly, to business queries to provide this context. In this section, we briefly state some directions for future research.

Using Business Queries to Surmise Context
Most business queries require the computation of information across business concepts. This computation often relies on *grouping* instances of a given business concept by common attributes (e.g., date of occurrence, location, participating entities, etc.) and, optionally, performing *aggregation* of

these or some other attributes of interest [Sismanis et al., 2009]. In our view, queries represent the best clues as to what information is of importance for vivification in BI.

Example 4.9   Consider the following business query: "How many patients have been admitted during the first quarter by speciality?." To answer this query we need to count (aggregate) the number of *distinct* patients (instances of business entity InPatient) per speciality (grouping condition), who have been hospitalized (instances of business process Admission) between January 1st and April 30th (range of interest). Notice how this simple query relies on complete information to provide meaningful and concrete answers: we must be able to distinguish inpatients from one another; we must be able to assert which medical specialty is in charge of treating each inpatient; and last, we must be able to differentiate between outpatient and inpatient registrations. If there are unknown or incomplete values, for example over the patient identifier, the query may not yield a correct complete answer. Similarly, in the presence of vivified attribute values, the query may yield a complete answer but it might not be the correct one. This might be the case, for instance, if we consider replacing any incomplete value in the specialty attribute by—symbolically—the most frequently used medical specialty in the hospital.

The previous example suggests there is an interaction between vivification and query answering, in particular when aggregation or grouping conditions involve vivified attributes. In some cases, the context of interpretation rendered by a vivification strategy may affect the response to a query. In some others, a given vivification strategy may be irrelevant to query answering. In our work, we recognize the importance of providing a context of interpretation that is authoritative for the purpose of answering business queries. The vivification of data should be driven by a business analyst's questions rather than by the initial necessary impulse of removing large amounts of inconsistencies or incompleteness in the data. Our last example suggests how this process could be systematically undertaken.

Example 4.10   In order to estimate the costs associated with frequent and potentially unavoidable hospital admissions, we are asked to monitor the rate with which hospital inpatients are being readmitted at any given time. While there is no one agreed-upon definition of the concept 'hospital readmissions' in the business schema, assume we are interested in those admission process instances which occur within five business days after discharge from an earlier hospitalization visit and, moreover, which cite the same reason for illness. Notice how the context of interpretation offered by this business query induces a *partial mapping* of data: we are no longer interested in mapping all hospital admissions and all possible inpatient instances, but only those instances which have the potential for causing readmissions. Intuitively, the vivification (or recognition) of admission process instances must acknowledge a new relationship at the business level, the one between a hospital admission and its related admission instances. The precise scope of this relationship depends on how we judge that any two inpatient admissions are due to the same reason of illness. While we may simply require matching (reason) attribute values, we may want to consider some domain specific facts describing known readmission causes, such as those readmissions arising due to post-surgical infections. Vivification must then bring forward this new semantic connection at the data level by making explicit relevant join and grouping conditions in the mapping.

Mining of Semantic Requirements from Business Process Models

In addition to using business queries, *business process models* are rich semantic sources for eliciting vivification assumptions. Indeed, within the specification of a business process model, we often encounter clues that can be exploited to aggregate event data. These *semantic clues* provide invaluable feedback to flesh out a collection of data events with additional information, in particular in those cases where we may have insufficient process instrumentation at the data level, or worse, data that do not realistically conform to idealized processes [van der Aalst, 2011].

Declarative Representation of Vivification Assumptions and Choices

Of extreme importance to vivification is the recording of any contextual assumptions used to interpret data, and any choices made during the data-to-business mapping process. The empirical evidence suggests that current BI/ETL tools offer little to no support for recording the thousand of choices made when confronted with incomplete and inconsistent information. These choices along with business rules are traditionally found buried deep in procedural scripts [Ross, 2001]. Instead, we argue that the recording should be done declaratively to enable automated reasoning and adaptation, and most importantly to permit the communication of assumptions and choices among teams of BI users.

A Holistic and Iterative Vivification Process

We have recently proposed a vision for solving the vivification problem in BI [Arocena et al., 2012]. In this vision, technologists and business users alike are involved in deploying and refining data-to-business solutions. We seek solutions to enable BI systems to be able to react to *real-time change*, such as changes in business policies and processes, and to graciously adapt any interpretation choices made so far in a timely fashion. In many business domains, our suggested vivification approach could greatly benefit from embracing alternative sources of knowledge such as text (e.g., e-mail), unstructured and semi-structured data (e.g., business guidelines), images (e.g., visual representations of process models), and so on. A holistic vivification approach for realizing all of these has yet to be proposed.

4.8   CONCLUSIONS

In this chapter, we have surveyed a wide variety of techniques for interpreting one database in terms of another. We have also proposed how to build on this foundation to provide an interpretation of operational data in business terms. In bridging the gap between the world of IT-supplied data and the world of business, we are working on a number of techniques for transforming operational data into complete high-quality business information. Current BI solutions tend to adopt a two-phase approach to solve this problem, where the mapping of data generally precedes the process of imparting a business semantics to it. In this chapter, we have advocated on-demand interpretation of IT-supplied data in terms of business concepts. Our work builds upon the foundation of knowledge base vivification [Levesque, 1986] and data exchange between disparate databases [Fagin et al., 2005a, Popa et al., 2002]. We have used a business model to represent business concepts, and schema mappings, from a database schema to a business model, to specify interpretations. We have reviewed a number of important research contributions in the literature, discussed issues, and highlighted potential solutions to the problem of vivifying incompleteness that arises due the lack of one-to-one correspondence between database-level, and business-level concepts.

Acknowledgements.   The authors wish to acknowledge Alex Borgida for his insightful comments and suggestions. This work was partially supported by the NSERC Business Intelligence Network.

CHAPTER 5

Information Integration in BI

Rachel A. Pottinger

5.1 INTRODUCTION

Today's businesses are overwhelmed with data coming from many different sources. A typical organization has hundreds of different data sources, whether they are formal databases or not. Consider the scenario in Example 5.1.

Example 5.1 A large retailer having many different stores may have payroll databases, transactions databases (e.g., when items were purchased in the store by whom), supply databases, customer databases, and many others. These databases are necessary for the business to function. However, the data from one database may need to be combined with data from other databases in order to fully answer all of the questions that the business users have: a business user from this company may want weekly reports on which stores, regions, and countries have sold how many products from various suppliers. This requires combining information from both the transactions and supply databases.

The desire to combine information from multiple sources is common, and given the increasing data available to today's business users, is both growing in demand and challenges. Applications requiring integration of data from multiple sources is known as *information integration*.

There are many other scenarios in which information integration is useful, such as those in the examples below.

Example 5.2 A medium-sized construction firm may have payroll databases, scheduling databases, cost estimation databases, building design files (e.g., CAD models), and many other data sources. The construction firm may be worried that costs on a project are going to overrun the estimate. In this case, just getting the information about the payroll implications alone needs to be drawn from scheduling and payroll databases, but getting all of the information is going to require also integrating information from text documents and other data sources.

Example 5.3 One of the great early triumphs of information integration comes from the airline industry and its reservation system, Sabre. Sabre allowed users (at first only skilled travel agents) to access data from many airline's different flight databases.

These scenarios all describe situations in which businesses can better fulfill their goals by combining information from different sources. However, they have different requirements. For example, the weekly reports required in Example 5.1 likely have much different accuracy and speed requirements, both in terms of application development and application performance, than the Sabre scenario in Example 5.3. In the rest of this chapter, we describe some of the common needs in information integration, where the requirements diverge, and what are some possible solutions.

The chapter is organized as follows. Section 5.2 describes a set of goals and axes on which we can compare information integration architectures. Section 5.3 describes some of the challenges that the information integration systems must overcome to achieve their goals. Section 5.4 describes some of the common information integration architectures, including data integration (Section 5.4.1), data warehousing (Section 5.4.2), and peer data management systems (PDMSs, Section 5.4.3). How the architectures compare on the axes is described in Section 5.2. Section 5.5 describes some of the ways in which these tools have impacted industry, and Section 5.6 concludes.

5.2   INFORMATION INTEGRATION GOALS AND AXES

While one could certainly imagine that the "perfect" information integration scenario would resolve all of these issues, currently there is no one architecture that is capable of handling all of these equally well. In this section we describe some of the common requirements for information integration, which we later match with existing information integration architectures and solutions.

Querying multiple sources simultaneously
All information integration problems have one thing in common: there are data that need to be combined from multiple datasets. As is shown in the introduction, there are many different cases and scenarios where this happens.

Speed of Development
Depending on the application and the needs of the companies involved, there will be a great variance in the amount of time that people are willing to wait to allow the information from various sources to be combined. For example, the construction firm in Example 5.2 may value getting a fast general answer to their overrun problems instead of getting the exact amounts correct.

On the other hand, Sabre (Example 5.3) is an example where the stakes are high enough so that the application designers were willing to wait a long time in order to integrate the data. While Sabre has undergone many different revisions now, the first iteration took seven years and 30 million dollars in order to create [Head, 2002]. So the amount of time and money that users are willing to invest is very different depending on the application. In the case of speed of development, the amount of time that users are willing to spend on development may vary substantially based on how often the types of queries can be reused.

Speed of Answering Queries

Another axis to consider is how fast it must be to answer queries. Here, again, there are many different standards. While it may seem at first that this is the same axis as the amount of time spent in development—after all, the longer one spends developing an application, the better chance there is that a faster application can be developed, the two are not always linked. For example, in the case of the large multinational retailer in Example 5.1, the information can be adequately processed on an overnight run. On the other hand, users waiting to book airline tickets (as in Example 5.3) will likely grow impatient in a few seconds.

Transactional Data Required

As updates are frequent, another issue to consider is whether the data that are being processed need to be current and up to date. For example, when reserving airline tickets (as in Example 5.3), it is extremely frustrating to get most of the way through the process only to discover that the price and/or availability of the tickets has changed. On the other hand, it is often feasible to allow users to review past sales data (as in Example 5.1) with data that are a day or two stale.

Precision of Responses

In most cases, all things being equal, people would rather get correct answers; it is better to get right answers than wrong ones. On the other hand, there are cases in information integration where having a fully correct answer may not be as important as it is in other cases. For example, in booking an air ticket (Example 5.3), the stakes are pretty high—there better be an available seat on board the airplane, or the airline is responsible for stiff fines. In other cases, the precision is not as important. For example, when trying to find large cost overruns in Example 5.2, having small errors in estimation does not cause a huge problem.

Flexibility

One big issue is whether the application requires much flexibility in terms of what answers are required. For example, in reserving an airline ticket (Example 5.3), there are expected to be a set number of request types. In managing retail stores (Example 5.1), there may be many different types of requests, but often centering around the same type of request: look at data from different sources at different levels of granularity. On the other hand, the construction firm in Example 5.2 may need to try many different types of queries to figure out their overruns.

Another type of flexibility is how easy it needs to be for new sources to be added to or to be removed from a system. This varies substantially across applications.

Desired Levels of Completeness

Another important axis is how complete the answer must be to be useful. Is there a need to have all of the information in order to make use of it, or is it sufficient to only have access to some information?

Types of Data Models

There are many different types of data models that might need to have data integrated in addition to the traditional relational databases. For example, continuing on with the construction firm example (Example 5.2), determining questions to other business problems, e.g., "if we lower the ceiling by 5cm in order to allow the general contractor to use a different construction method, what other aspects of the design are impacted?" will involve data sources that are not relational. In this case, a CAD model (or its successor, a Building Information Model (BIM)) must be integrated with the other data.

Axis Summary

As noted, there are many different kinds of axes that must be considered. In the next section we describe some of the different information integration architectures. We then proceed to discuss how well they adhere to the different axes presented.

5.3 CHALLENGES AND BACKGROUND

In this section we describe some of the challenges that must be overcome to allow the necessary integration to occur, and along the way define some of the terms needed to describe the problems and their solution fully.

5.3.1 SCHEMAS AND SEMANTIC HETEROGENEITY

One of the big problems in information integration is semantic heterogeneity. For example, if all of the information about flights is to be combined from a set of different flight databases (as in Example 5.3), then the different databases are likely to have different representations of flight information. The way in which this information is stored is referred to as a *schema*. For the purposes of this chapter, we generally restrict our discussion to relational databases, but the same principles can be applied to an XML document.

For example, continuing with flight information, we can imagine that there might be a relation Airport with two attributes, Code and City. The relation will contain a set of *tuples* describing individual "Airports" which are defined by their Code and City, denoted Airports(Code,City). Figure 5.1 shows two instances of Airports: The airport in Vancouver has the airport code YVR, and the airport for Toronto has the airport code YYZ.

Code	City
DCA	Washington DC
IAD	Washington DC
YVR	Vancouver
YYZ	Toronto

Figure 5.1: Example relation instance for the Airport relation.

A semantic heterogeneity problem occurs when users attempt to integrate data from two databases with two different schemas. For example, one airline may store information about airports in the relation in Figure 5.1, and another may store it in the relation AirportInfo(City, Country, ThreeLetterCode, Latitude, Longitude). If a business user wants to be able to answer questions that involve both sources (e.g., to find the cheapest flights between two cities, regardless of which airline the flights are on), information must be passed between the two schemas. There must be some representation that allows users to query both databases simultaneously.

5.3.2 ONTOLOGIES

Many business information integration scenarios will involve integrating ontologies. An *ontology* is a specification of a vocabulary about a domain and a set of relationships between objects in the domain [Fikes, 1996]. While there are a number of different types of ontologies (see Biemann [2005] for a categorization), most ontologies contain relationships such as ISA and HASA between elements in the ontology. For example, an ontology about financial instruments may say that an "Issued Share" ISA "Share." Consider the following example that uses an ontology to provide better integration.

Example 5.4 Consider a bank that is trying to analyze the relationships between all of its different types of accounts in order to better make decisions. There are different types of databases for different types of accounts—the information about savings accounts are stored in very different databases from those discussing stock market investments. In order to integrate the information, they must first be able to tell what the relationships are between the elements in the different databases. Doing so may be done by an ontology such as the Financial Industry Business Ontology (FIBO) [EDM Council, 2011] which describes the relationships between elements.

5.4 OVERVIEW OF DIFFERENT INFORMATION INTEGRATION ARCHITECTURES

5.4.1 DATA INTEGRATION

In data integration, a number of data sources are left as independent entities, but queried together using a single, *mediated schema* on which to answer the queries.

For example, consider the scenario in Figure 5.2, which is drawn from an airline scenario, like that in Example 5.3. Each data source (e.g., British Airways and Air Canada) has its own database.

Since the data have not been stored in the mediated schema, user queries must be *reformulated* into queries over the local sources that store the data. The query reformulator then looks in the data source catalog to find sources that are relevant to the query, as in the typical data integration architecture shown in Figure 5.3 [Levy et al., 1996b].

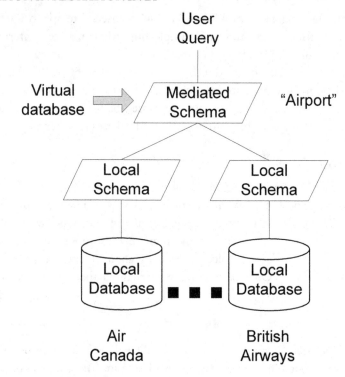

Figure 5.2: Typical data integration example.

Continuing with the scenario in Figure 5.2, the user would ask a query over the mediated schema's relation "airline," which would be translated into the corresponding concepts in the British Airways and Air Canada schemas.

A system catalog stores which source has which data. This information is often stored using views. For example, early architectures tended to define the global source as a view (i.e., saved queries) upon the local sources (see [Lenzerini, 2002] for a survey), which was difficult to add sources to. Later works chose an approach where either local sources were defined as views upon the global schema [Levy et al., 1996b], or views could be defined in either direction [Friedman et al., 1999]. In both of the latter cases, adding or removing sources was as simple as adding or removing views describing the relevant sources from the system catalog.

After the system reformulates the query over the mediated schema into queries over the sources (including figuring out which part of the query to ask over which source) [Duschka and Genesereth, 1997, Pottinger and Halevy, 2001], these queries are sent out to the various sources to be executed, and the results are combined and returned to the user [Ives et al., 1999].

Because the sources are independent, they may follow different data models—or scraped from the web. In this case, the wrappers will help translate between the source's original data model and

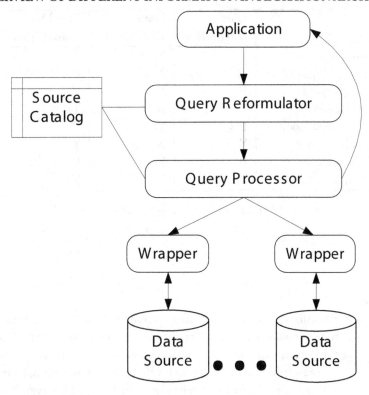

Figure 5.3: Typical data integration architecture as in [Levy et al., 1996b].

the one used by the data integration system. In some cases (e.g., relational local sources and an XML mediated schema) this is quite simple, where as in others (e.g., HTML to relational) it is more challenging [Gruser, 1998, Hammer et al., 1997, Kushmerick et al., 1997].

Data Integration on the Axes

Figure 5.4 shows how the various architectures meet some of the pressures required by business intelligence information integration architectures. As we can see, data integration does quite well on a number of these. As with all of the architectures in this chapter, it allows users to query multiple sources. Thanks to the wrappers, it is possible to have multiple data models be integrated at the same time. Data integration is also capable of handling transactional data since the transactional data sources themselves are what are queried at query time. Finally, adding and removing sources is simple thanks to the view-based systems catalog.

	Data Integration	Data Warehouses	Peer Data Management Systems
Multiple sources	Y	Y	Y
Fast development	N	N	P
Fast querying	P	Y	P
Transactional data	Y	N	Y
Provides precision	P	Y	P
Flexible sources	Y	N	Y
Completeness	P	Y	P
Multiple datamodels	Y	N	Y

Figure 5.4: Comparing the different architectures on the different axes. The entries are "Yes," "Partial," or "No."

Completeness

Data integration partially succeeds at providing complete answers. In particular, this is because a data integration system makes what is referred to as the *open world assumption*. Informally, this means that while the data in a data source are assumed to be correct, even if a data source contains a relation, it does not necessarily contain *all* tuples for that relation. For example, in the Sabre example (Example 5.3), each airline probably has a relation about flights. However, it is not assumed that each database has information about *all* flights from all airlines, and there may be some airlines with flights that are not represented in the integration system at all. However, it is assumed that the information that does appear about flights is correct.

Therefore, the goal of the data integration system is to answer queries the best that it can given the sources available. This notion of doing the best possible given the information available is known as returning all *certain answers* [Abiteboul and Duschka, 1998].

Thus, data integration systems are able to provide partially complete answers. The system guarantees that it will provide the best answer given the sources available. However, it does not assume that it will have access to all such answers.

Querying Speed

Data integration systems are able to quickly answer simple queries as long as (1) the mediator is not much of a bottleneck, (2) the data sources are responsive, (3) there is not too much network delay. It is true that in two of the architectures that data integration systems commonly used, where at least some of the sources are represented as views over the mediated schema, rewriting queries is NP complete [Levy et al., 1995]. However, in practical situations rewriting the queries has been shown to be quite tractable [Pottinger and Halevy, 2001].

However, processing complex queries requiring lots of aggregation will be slow—the results are not pre-computed and they must be reprocessed each time the query is processed.

Development Speed

Data integration systems are relatively slow to set up, primarily because creating the mediated schema and performing the initial system is quite slow. Typically, a mediated schema is created by hand, and thus quite slow.

On the other hand, adding sources to the systems where the local sources are modeled as views over the mediated schema is fairly rapid—it only requires adding a few sets of Datalog rules to the list of mappings in the source catalog [Levy et al., 1996a]. While this problem can itself be complex (as seen in the previous chapter), once the mappings are created, it is almost instantaneous to begin querying the new sources.

Adoption

Data integration works quite well in the business intelligence context, and as shown in Section 5.5, it has been well adopted by industry. One reason that data integration works so well for business intelligence is that the amount of time that is needed to set up a good data integration system, including building the mappings and the mediated schema, can be offset by the reuse of the system over time. Business users are well motivated to create these systems, even though the development is slow. In today's business intelligence context, the push is on to provide tools that are more nimble and flexible. The challenge for data integration will be how to create systems that allow for similarly precise answers but requires less development time.

5.4.2   DATA WAREHOUSING

In contrast to data integration, in data warehousing the data are gathered into a central repository, as shown in Figure 5.5. The data are first extracted from the sources, then cleansed and transformed into the representation needed by the data warehouse, and finally loaded into the data warehouse.

A data warehouse will typically allow users to explore various aspects of the data, known as *dimensions*, each of which has a hierarchy showing the different levels of granularity that the business analyst might be interested in.

For example, in the case of the large retailer in Example 5.1, the schema may include a dimension for time, which shows various levels of granularity, including day, month, and year, as shown in Figure 5.6.

The data in a data warehouse are often organized in a data cube [Gray et al., 1996], which allows the data to be retrieved easily by looking for data that is represented in the different dimensions. For example, Figure 5.7 shows a partial representation of the sales data in Figure 5.6. Each cell within the cube represents sales of a specific product at a specific time at specific locations.

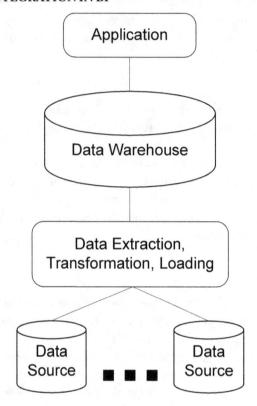

Figure 5.5: Typical data warehousing architecture.

Because these data may need be to analyzed at different levels of granularity, data warehouses often offer the opportunity to either look more deeply at the data, called *drilling down* (e.g., starting from all the sales in December 2011, the user may drill down and look at the sales on individual days of December 2011), or to look at the data at a higher level of granularity (e.g., starting from the December 2011 data, the business analyst may want to look at all of the data aggregated over 2011).

Data Warehousing on the Axes

Comparing data warehousing with the axes in Figure 5.4, we can see that there are many things that data warehouses excel at. Their prowess is largely thanks to their gathering all the data in one place, which is not the case in any of the other information architectures considered in this chapter. In particular, data warehouses are quite good at answering queries, provide precise data, and also are assumed to be complete.

On the other hand, their reliance on storing data in the warehouse means that they are slow to develop, are inappropriate for querying transactional data (the transactions must take place on

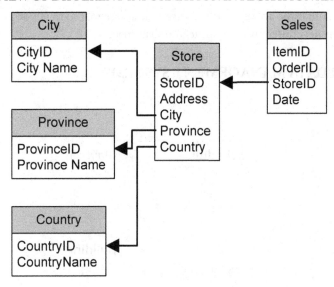

Figure 5.6: Sample warehousing schema for some of the information in Example 5.1.

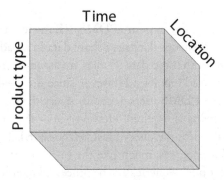

Figure 5.7: Sample data cube built from some of the dimensions of Figure 5.6.

the original data), are very inflexible, and require that all the data be in—or able to be transformed into—the same data model.

Adoption

Business Intelligence is the killer application for data warehouses: business users are motivated to create the most precise data repositories possible in order to better make their business decisions. In today's context, however, their inflexibility is a challenge. In order to continue to be successful in future business intelligence applications, methods will need to be created to allow sources to be added more easily. An additional challenge is to materialize only part of the warehouse: with the onslaught of data that the average business user has access to, too much of a data warehouse may be computed that is never used, wasting time and disk space.

5.4.3   PEER DATA MANAGEMENT SYSTEMS

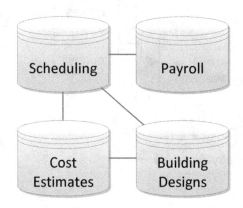

Figure 5.8: Sample PDMS architecture.

In a peer data management system (PDMS) [Bernstein et al., 2002, Halevy et al., 2003], multiple independent, heterogeneous databases share data in an ad hoc manner. A PDMS is like a peer to peer (P2P) network in that the data sources are assumed to be able to come and go as they please and there is often no fixed topology. However, since the databases are independent, they may have their own schemas. In a PDMS users generally query the data in the PDMS using their own schema, so no mediated schema is required. However, in order for results from one database to be passed to another, the data and/or the query must be translated. To resolve this issue, mappings are required between the various sources, much like the ones in data integration systems. In general, these mappings are bi-directional—queries can be processed in either direction. Query processing is more complicated than in data integration, since answering queries may require composing mappings between sources in order to answer questions.

Figure 5.8 shows a sample PDMS based on the disaster scenario in Example 5.2. The lines show the mappings that exist between the sources. Because Scheduling has mappings to all of the other three sources, queries between it and any of the other sources can be translated directly. This means that business intelligence users can easily ask questions relating to any scheduling issues, allowing them to more flexibly schedule their workers and thus improve efficiency. However, queries between Payroll and Cost Estimates must be routed through Scheduling. Queries from Payroll to Building Designs have two options. Either they can go from Payroll to Scheduling Building Designs, or they can go from Payroll to Scheduling to Cost Estimates to Building Designs. Depending on the quality of the mappings, there may be additional answers that can be retrieved using the longer route, so both translation options may be explored.

PDMSs on the axes

Because PDMSs share many of the same characteristics of data integration (e.g., the data is left in the independent sources, and queries are translated via the mappings), the PDMS entry in Figure 5.4 looks much like the one for data integration.

The key difference is that PDMSs allow faster development than data integration systems. This is because the data integration system requires a mediated schema, which is slow to create, and PDMSs do not require a mediated schema.

While both are, indeed, flexible, the PDMS is more flexible than a data integration system since, unlike the other architectures under consideration, they do not require a centralized authority. Additionally, the PDMS is more flexible in adding sources, since the source may decide to add a mapping to any of the other sources available.

Adoption

Unlike data integration and data warehouses, PDMSs have not seen much success in business intelligence. A chief stumbling block is that PDMSs require too much effort to create given the relatively low level of precision that they provide. One issue is that since most PDMSs only allow users to query over the schema of one of the sources, it is quite difficult to leverage the infrastructure created in order to answer some complex queries that require accessing pieces of data that appear only in a limited number of sources. Additionally, since business users are motivated to find the most precise (and potentially the most complicated) answers, an architecture which still requires a fair amount of work to create but does not provide good guarantees provides the wrong incentives: for business intelligence, something that illuminates the point quickly is useful, and something that provides details is useful, but PDMSs fall on a point in the spectrum that is a hard fit for business users.

5.5   INFORMATION INTEGRATION TOOLS IN INDUSTRY

Due to the large demand for such tools, many are being incorporated into industry. Data warehouses, the first of the technologies here to reach markets, have been developed by most of the big players in databases, such as IBM, Microsoft, and Oracle.

Data integration systems met with a name change on their way to being implemented in industry, and are typically known in industry as *enterprise information integration (EII)* systems [Halevy et al., 2005]. These systems have been developed by a number of established companies, such as IBM's InfoSphere Information Server.[1] EII was also pursued by a number of start-ups in the 1990s, such as Nimble [Draper et al., 2001], which were bought by other companies, and others, such as Informatica,[2] which remain major players in EII today. A summary of some of the major players is given by Halevy et al. [2005].

---

[1]http://www-01.ibm.com/software/data/integration/info_server/overview.html
[2]http://www.informatica.com/us/

A related problem is that of *enterprise application integration (EAI)* systems, which focus on integrating *applications* rather than *data* [Linthicum, 2000].

5.6   CONCLUSIONS

As shown in Figure 5.4, there is (currently) no one type of semantic integration architecture that is capable of achieving well on all of the axes that business analysts may desire in integrating their data. Indeed, there are many trade-offs. The biggest distinction between the various types of integration platforms is between warehouses—which archive all of the data in one place—and the remaining systems. Because of this archiving, the warehouses are able to answer queries quickly and also make good claims about completeness. However, they cannot provide the flexibility and the ease of development that the other systems can provide.

CHAPTER 6

Information Extraction for BI

Denilson Barbosa, Luiz Gomes, Jr., and Frank Wm. Tompa

6.1 INTRODUCTION

BI consists of using analytical tools to derive actionable information from business data, with the goal of supporting strategic decisions. As discussed so far, the data used in such analyses are usually highly structured and stored in relational databases. However, this misses a wealth of unstructured data which are harder to integrate but can provide valuable information. Sources for such data include formal documents, reports, exchanged messages, and numerous websites on the Internet. *Information Extraction* (*IE*) from text, also called *text analytics*, is the process of turning unstructured information embedded in texts into structured data [Jurafsky, 2008], which can then be integrated into the BI process.

According to folklore 80% of all information used within corporations for decision making is *unstructured* [Kuechler, 2007], being recorded in audio-visual formats, and, especially, as text. There are many key business applications where primarily textual information is critical for BI. Customer management, for instance, relies on recording and analyzing feedback often in textual form: email communications, transcripts of phone conversations, and even activity in social media sites. In the medical domain, the vast majority of the relevant information is captured around text: historical patient records mix numeric information (e.g., results of tests) with descriptions of symptoms for the different visits to the hospital. Another concern of modern business is compliance with government regulations, which are also provided as extensive textual content. Other forms of less structured data are prevalent in modern business operations: spreadsheets and web data are two examples.

While there are many applications of unstructured and partially structured data in BI, there are also many challenges in dealing with such data. Perhaps the biggest one is that of *terminology*. Unlike with structured databases, which come with explicit and detailed schemas, the specification of the meaning of unstructured data is implicit with text. Within IE, a great deal of effort goes into adding semantic annotations to the text, in order to apply the extraction algorithms per se. One common theme is the use of existing semantic structures (e.g., public online databases or knowledge bases such as Wikipedia) to achieve this goal. Once the documents are enriched with semantics, structured data can be extracted, analyzed, and integrated within the usual BI lifecycle of the organization.

This chapter focuses on applying IE to extract structured data from unstructured and semi-structured sources consisting primarily of text. There are two main schools of IE. Within the natural language processing (NLP) community, the focus has been more on extracting information from natural language (e.g., noun phrases that answer a "why" question), and employing deeper linguistic analysis that build on text semantics. This is the subject of Section 6.2. In the database community, on the other hand, the focus has been on extracting structured data from websites by relying on syntactic clues in the texts' markup, and this is the subject of Section 6.3. Despite these prima facie differences, both approaches aim at identifying and exploiting statistically significant *patterns* that reveal actionable information. Moreover, the cross-fertilization across communities has recently intensified. Before describing those techniques, however, the remainder of this section includes a more thorough look at the nature of data and the role of IE for BI. The chapter concludes with additional approaches to including IE as part of BI.

6.1.1   LEVELS OF STRUCTUREDNESS

The term *structured data* refers to data that adhere to a *formal* (database) model. The importance of structure in data cannot be overstated. Structure allows the unambiguous retrieval of information and provides clear semantics to computations on the data. Strictly speaking, *unstructured* means completely lacking formal organization (i.e., structure). To say any real data are unstructured is hardly appropriate as only a truly random sequence of symbols can be considered fully devoid of structure. For example, sentences in natural language follow grammatical rules that make them far from random sequences of letters. Nevertheless, it must be noted that while grammatical rules are in fact formal, they are not *data* models. Moreover, they do not preclude ambiguity: perfectly valid sentences may have more than one meaning [Raymond et al., 1996]. To make matters worse, not all text fragments fully comply with grammar rules. A more useful definition of unstructured data is thus data that do not conform to a structured data model, and thus cannot be queried nor processed directly by analytics systems.

One advantage of having structured data is that it can be described easily by means of a concise *schema*. Almost invariably, the schema is several orders of magnitude smaller than the actual data (e.g., describing a few hundred tables with several million tuples in them). This leads to a useful characterization of degree of the structuredness in data: structured data are unambiguous and have schemas that are much smaller than the data, whereas unstructured data are ambiguous and would require schemas as large as or larger than the data themselves. Another kind of data is known as *semi-structured data*, which, as the name suggests, are neither fully structured nor fully unstructured. The term has often been used to describe data where not all of their "elements" fully comply with a fixed schema, or data whose schema requires too many rules and exceptions for the data to be compliant.

The distinction between unstructured and semi-structured is not crisp, however. Typically, even unstructured data come with *metadata*, such as the email address of the user who wrote an online review of a product, or the model of a digital camera used for a picture. Consider now email messages, which consist of a mix of structured and unstructured fields: the body of the message will contain mostly text (unstructured), whereas the sender and recipients are clearly specified (structured). In the context of BI, common examples of unstructured data encompass primarily textual content (e.g., reports, news articles, blog posts, legislation) as well as other forms of media (e.g., charts, presentations, voice, images, and video). Semi-structured data sources include so-called *structured documents* (e.g., email, Wikipedia articles with fact boxes, product reviews), in which many elements are unambiguously delimited although their content is mostly unstructured (e.g., text).

6.1.2   THE ROLE OF IE FOR BI

IE applies to unstructured and semi-structured data. Ultimately, its goal is to identify and exploit underlying or implicit structure in the data, so as to *derive* a fully structured representation of the data that can be analyzed (e.g., by standard BI tools). This vision can be operationalized in two major ways: extending traditional cube/OLAP systems with primitives to handle documents, or applying IE as a "pre-processing" step, where structured data are extracted, and analyzing the results with standard BI tools. In either case, care must be taken so that the provenance of any information derived from unstructured content is not lost.

Extending the OLAP Cube

The first approach is well exemplified by the work of Lin et al. [2008], who propose the Text Cube model, which is a data cube with a new dimension (called *term hierarchy*) and associated operations to allow semantic navigation of the data based on keywords and their relationship. Tseng and Chou [2006] define dimensions for document data that can encompass document metadata (such as author, subject, publisher, etc), keywords, summaries, and category classification. Summarization and keyword extraction are automated in the proposal. The defining characteristic of these approaches is that the result of the analysis returns documents.

Another example where IE is applied to extract structured data to help in BI is the work of Pérez-Martínez et al. [2008], describing a system comprising a document warehouse and a traditional data warehouse. They identify *links* to the facts in the data warehouse's fact table within the documents in the document warehouse, thus using the unstructured data to provide *context* for the BI task. In this approach, analysis starts with the user specifying a *context* by supplying a sequence of keywords. Then a *Relevance Cube* (R-cube) is materialized by retrieving both documents and facts related to the context.

IE As Pre-processing

A more data-driven approach to the integration of documents in the analysis process is to apply information extraction tools to handle specific data needs. If an analyst knows precisely what information is required and where it can be found, IE extraction systems can be adapted to suit the needs. This approach resembles the familiar *Extract-Transform-Load* (*ETL*) workflow outlined in Chapter 2, having unstructured or semi-structured sources as its starting point.

Saggion et al. [2007] adapt the GATE language engineering system [Cunningham et al., 2011] to handle BI tasks over textual sources. They employ ontologies to represent target concepts,

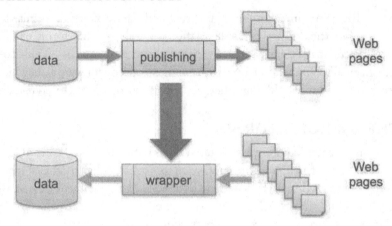

Figure 6.1: Wrapper induction from web pages coming from a structured source.

and discuss techniques to address extraction tasks for company profiles, country and region facts, and financial statements.

Another approach, more suitable for semi-structured Web content, is described by Baumgartner et al. [2001], who apply their Lixto System in the BI scenario. The mechanisms in the system mimic standard ETL tools, facilitating usage by data warehouse professionals. The extraction process begins with the specification of *wrappers* (illustrated in Figure 6.1), through the use of an interactive user interface. The wrapper agents are then embedded in the runtime environment of the transformation service, where the extracted data can be aggregated, re-formatted and delivered. The authors showcase two applications for monitoring product prices in a market. There is no mention of specific requirements that distinguish the BI scenario from any other IE task.

Structure and Meaning

It should be clear that understanding text (at the human level) is far beyond the capabilities of current artificial intelligence and NLP tools. In a sense, the goal of IE is to provide a means to bridge the gap between the analytics tools that require structured data and the unstructured nature of text, which contains a wealth of useful information. Conceptually, this happens by inferring latent structure in the text, which is then *mapped* to a (structured) database schema. Facts derived from the text are then made into tuples in the database, and the analytics tools are then applied seamlessly.

Broadly speaking, IE addresses the identification of classes (or concepts), entities (or instances), and relations among those entities. Intuitively, classes and relations are mapped into the database schema, and the instances of such classes and relations become the tuples that make up the database.

NP "such as" NP*
cities such as London, Paris, and Rome

"such" NP "as" NP* "or" | "and" NP
works by such authors as Herrick and Shakespeare

NP, NP* "or" | "and other" NP
bruises, wounds broken bones or other injuries

NP "especially" | "including" NP*
all common-law countries including Canada and England

Figure 6.2: Example of extraction patterns [Hearst, 1992].

6.2   IE FROM TEXT

Information Extraction is a long-standing challenge in NLP that was strongly revived with the advent and popularization of the web. The goal here is to extract information from natural language; this is done by understanding and exploiting the ways in which natural language is used to express information. Whereas most of the tools and techniques apply to any corpus, many recent methods were designed with the web in mind or to explore resources on the web, such as Wikipedia.

The advent of the web, and its size, help in several ways. First, the web provides meaningful notions of support: true facts are likely to be repeated several times on the web. Also, the web enables *distant supervision*: we can rely on known facts to extract new ones. Finally, the web allows us to gather contextual clues by looking at other resources.

Terminology
It is useful to define basic knowledge representation terminology to illustrate the discussion.

Definition 6.1   Concepts (or classes) are placeholders for sets of instances (or objects). For example, book, author, city, company, and university are concepts.

Definition 6.2   Instances (or objects) are elements of the sets named by the concepts. Examples

of concepts with their respective instance sets are:

book ={The Book Thief, War Horse, Calico Joe, Pride and Prejudice, Emma, . . .}
author ={Markus Zusak, Michael Morpurgo, John Grisham, Jane Austen, . . .}

Definition 6.3   Relations are sets of connected instances, usually from different concepts. Examples:

$$author\text{-}of\text{-}book = \{(Markus\ Zusak,\ The\ Book\ Thief),\ (Michael\ Morpurgo,\ War\ Horse),$$
$$(John\ Grisham,\ Calico\ Joe),\ (Jane\ Austen,\ Pride\ and\ Prejudice),$$
$$(Jane\ Austen,\ Emma),\ \dots\}$$

Binary relations relate exactly two concepts (as in the author-of-book example), whereas n-ary relations involve, as the name suggests, n concepts. From a knowledge representation point of view, this distinction is significant: in a strict sense, representation systems based on binary relations are less expressive than those that use n-ary relations. However, binary systems augmented with *reification* (as present in RDF) can emulate more expressive representation frameworks. Most current IE systems extract binary relations only; n-ary relations are identified from a set of binary associations as a post-processing step.

6.2.1   PATTERNS IN LANGUAGE

As discussed above, IE from text consists of identifying and exploiting patterns found in the way natural language text is composed. The difficulty of the process is that the number of patterns is very large, and the set of applicable patterns depends on the kind of content, the style of the author, and also the quality of the text. To contrast two extremes, consider extracting information from a comprehensive news article, written by a professional journalist, who was trained in writing and provides factual descriptions of events in clear and accessible language, versus extracting information from a 140-character-long Twitter post.

Hearst Patterns

One truly remarkable phenomenon that enables several IE tools is that there is a rather succinct list of patterns through which *hyponyms* (i.e., sub-concepts or instances of a concept) are expressed in natural language text. A canonical example is the pattern

$$NP_1\ \text{"such as"}\ NP_2*,$$

in which NP_1 represents a noun phrase and NP_2* represents a list of noun-phrases. A concrete instantiation of this rule is "cities such as London, Paris, and Rome," by which one is able to identify instances of the concept **city**.

Hearst [1992] observed this fact, and identified a list of patterns that can be used to extract hyponyms in text. Figure 6.2 shows a few more examples of such patterns. These patterns illustrate where structure can be found in "unstructured" data, as discussed before: not only is hyponymy expressed using these patterns, but also these patterns express hyponymy and nothing else. The impact of Hearst's observations is that they are "universal": in fact, they have been used and improved time and again with success. Moreover, they are also very robust: entire information extraction systems, such as KnowItAll [Etzioni et al., 2004], have been built predicated on these kinds of patterns.

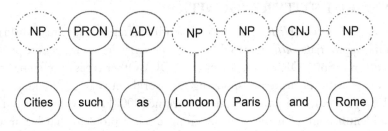

Figure 6.3: Labeled sequence with parts of speech.

Sequence Labeling

It should be noted that the original formulation of Hearst patterns, as discussed in the previous section, is inherently syntactic: the presence of the words "such as," in this order, are part of the pattern. Indeed, a naive implementation of an instance extractor based on Hearst's observations would start by finding occurrences of the words "such as" in the text, then identifying the list to its right, and the class name to its left.

This purely syntactic approach constitutes an example of what is known as a *shallow NLP* tool: there is no substantial language processing, only exact matching at the string level. A more sophisticated implementation would be to use a semantic parser that would provide an interpretation of the sentence according to a grammar (in this case for the English language). In fact, the idea has been generalized to use parts of speech and also dependency graphs formed over the words in a sentence, as the basis for defining the patterns for information extraction [Snow et al., 2005].

The downside of using *deep NLP* processing is its computational cost. Most tasks in understanding natural language are computationally demanding, and they are often too expensive to be deployed in large scale. Semantic parsing is among the most expensive as it turns out. Fortunately, various kinds of language processing steps are possible, offering different compromises in terms of cost/benefit. For instance, one popular analysis that is not very costly is to assign a part of speech (*POS*) tag to each word in the sentence, as illustrated in Figure 6.3. Observe that identifying the class and the instances once such POS tags are assigned becomes more straightforward.

A prominent approach is to view POS-tagging as a *sequence prediction* problem, where a stochastic model is built over a sample of annotated sentences and applied to predict the tags of unseen sentences. Conditional Random Fields (CRF) [Lafferty et al., 2001] are the state-of-the-art in stochastic POS-tagging, and have been shown to be far superior to previous methods, both in terms of accuracy and computational cost to the point that they have been deployed at web scale for tasks such as entity and relation extraction. Diesner and Carley [2008] show how to use conditional random fields on sequences of annotated text to extract entities and classify them into categories.

6.2.2   NAMED ENTITY RECOGNITION

Named Entity Recognition (*NER*) is the task of identifying references to real world entities in the text and assigning appropriate *entity tags* to those references. Typical examples are persons' names (using tag PER), organizations (ORG), and locations (LOC). Other types of references, such as dates and monetary values with no clear corresponding real world entity (e.g., Monday, $25,000), have also been tackled by NER techniques. Nadeau and Sekine [2007] survey the research in NER.

The identification of named entities from text is a problem that has received a great deal of attention. There are two main approaches to the problem: *closed-domain*, which corresponds to extracting instances of a given concept, and *open domain*, which corresponds to identifying both the concepts and the instances. In both cases, supervised methods have been used successfully. In the case of closed-domain extraction, the training data usually consist of a few example instances, whereas for open-domain extraction the training is usually at the meta-level: examples of sentences that contain classes and instances are given.

Another broad way of dividing NER methods is based on whether they rely on hand-crafted rules or statistical machine learning techniques. A simple rule to identify persons' names is to look for the title "Mr." followed by capitalized words. A learning-based approach aims at learning such rules automatically from annotated training data. Rule-based approaches are computationally efficient, but may miss out on many subtleties and are hard to adapt to new domains. Adapting a learning-based system to a new domain requires no changes in the algorithms, but it requires adequate amounts of training data.

Both rule and learning-based systems require the identification of features that characterize references to the entities. Features can be harvested from several characteristics of the text, such as word morphology, grammar, and sentence context. An adequate choice of features can be as important as the choice of technique to be used [Tjong Kim Sang and De Meulder, 2003].

NER systems often employ lists of terms to produce features. For example, the presence of a word in a list of common first names is highly indicative of a reference to a person and can be used as a feature. Lists of stop words, dictionaries of names, and gazetteers of places are examples of resources used in several NER tasks. Looking up terms in lists also defines an entire subtask in NER: when the names of potential entities are known beforehand, the system has to match the names in the text. The main challenges in this case are (i) references to entities can diverge from the canonical name in the list, and (ii) names vary in the number of tokens, which explodes the number of candidate substrings to be tested in each document.

Ananthanarayanan et al. [2008] address the first problem in the context of product names. The authors encode rules that generate synonyms to expand the dictionary of products. The rules are domain-specific, deriving synonyms by removing common prefixes or suffixes and extracting acronyms.

Capturing the rules that generate synonyms is a challenging task, especially considering the uncontrolled web environment. Chaudhuri et al. [2009] also address the product name domain, but exploit a document corpus to identify variations on how the entities are mentioned. The authors

[PER Michelle Obama] told [PER Ray] that the family will likely watch the game over a plate of nachos and a side of guacamole, favorite [MISC Super Bowl] snacks.

As for who the first family may be rooting for, President [PER Obama] told [ORG ABC News]' [PER Diane Sawyer] that he "can't call it" because he risks getting into trouble.

"When the [LOC Chicago] [ORG Bears] are not involved, I can't make predictions because I will get into trouble," [PER Obama] said last month, referring to his favorite hometown football team.

...

While [PER Obama] is staying on the sidelines, Vice President [PER Joe Biden] hasn't been bashful about offering his take.

Figure 6.4: Sentences tagged with named entities, where MISC represents other entity types.

rely on the observations that (i) terms are often dropped in product mentions (e.g., "Microsoft Office 2000" vs. "Office 2000"), and (ii) the dropped terms are often mentioned in other parts of the document so that the shortened mention can be disambiguated.

The idea behind the algorithm is, for each entity in the reference table, to find mentions omitting some tokens and to assess their correlation with the original entity based on the presence of the missing tokens in other parts of the document. The authors aim at employing a very large corpus (tens of terabytes) to extract the synonyms. To cope with the load, the system employs indexes for candidate synonyms and partial results. Furthermore, to minimize the number of string comparisons, the authors develop a filter that first prunes the substrings that cannot be candidates.

Figure 6.4 shows an excerpt from a news article,[1] tagged with named entities by a state-of-the-art tool, the Illinois NER system [Ratinov and Roth, 2009]. Several facts are evident from the tags in that example. For instance, several instances of various classes are extracted: Michelle Obama and Joe Biden for Person, Chicago for Location, and ABC News for Organization. Other facts can be derived with the help of background knowledge. For instance, if one is aware of the concept "Vice President," one can infer that Joe Biden is an instance, through the application of a simple textual pattern. Similarly, one can infer that Obama is an instance of "President" (sentence 2).

Co-Reference Resolution and Entity Linking
While many facts can be extracted in the example above, many more facts could be derived through further processing of the text. For example, the third sentence says that the favorite football team of President Obama is the Chicago Bears. This information can be inferred if one understands that the possessive determiner "his" at the end of the sentence *refers* to the Person Obama *and* that the Person Obama in that sentence *refers* to the instance of President in the previous sentence.

[1] http://abcnews.go.com/blogs/politics/2012/02/super-bowl-at-the-white-house-a-family-affair-in-2012/

Co-reference resolution is the task of resolving references within and across sentences in text. Usually, co-reference resolution is applied as a post-processing step after named entities have been identified. Orthomatcher [Bontcheva et al., 2002] is one intra-document co-reference resolution tool provided by the GATE framework. It is a rule-based system based on shallow NLP methods, which are inexpensive and ad-hoc, but often shown to perform well in many tasks. Orthomatcher relies on gazetteers, a lexicon of common abbreviations (Ltd., Inc., etc.), and a list of synonyms (New York = "the big apple," Edmonton = "the city of champions," etc.); it can also be made to use ad-hoc lists for a specific domain. The co-reference resolution of proper names follows orthographical matches (e.g., James Jones = Mr. Jones) and considers token re-ordering and abbreviations (University of Sheffield = Sheffield U.). By default, the rules can be applied transitively, although non-transitivity and exclusion triggers exist for some rules (e.g., to avoid matching "BBC News" to "News"). For co-reference resolution of pronouns, Orthomatcher relies on ad-hoc grammar rules, substantiated by empirical observation (e.g., 80% of all uses of 'he,' 'his,' 'she,' and 'her' refer to the closest person in the text).

Raghunathan et al. [2010] propose a multi-pass, unsupervised method in which several co-reference resolution rules are applied, in order. The authors observe that even some high-recall rules can lead to incorrect resolution if applied directly because of false positive matches. However, applying rules that cover rarer co-resolution cases first leads to drastically reducing the number of mis-applied rules, resulting in a much better accuracy overall.

Traditional co-reference resolution methods are inherently *intra*-document, relying on clues within each document separately. One limitation of this approach is that it may lead to incorrect resolutions. In the example in Figure 6.4, a system such as Orthomatcher would likely resolve entities Michelle Obama and (President) Obama as referring to the same person, because of their proximity and lexical similarity. External knowledge can avoid this problem, however. For instance, Wikipedia has an article on President Obama, which refers to Michelle Obama as a separate entity (his wife). This knowledge can prevent the incorrect conclusion that Michelle Obama is the same as President Obama. Moreover, such information is stored on Wikipedia in a relatively easy format to process, namely in *infoboxes*.

We can go one step further beyond preventing an incorrect inference, which is to annotate every occurrence of President Obama in the original document with a unique ID corresponding to the actual President (e.g., a link to the corresponding Wikipedia article). Linking mentions to entities in text to real-world entities in a knowledge base or external corpus such as Wikipedia has become an active topic of research lately. Ratinov et al. [2011] describe a method for such a task that extends classical work on word sense disambiguation by exploiting the graph structure of concepts and articles provided by Wikipedia. Milne and Witten [2008] use machine learning to link terms in a text to their corresponding Wikipedia articles, achieving recall and precision around 75%.

While much still remains to be done in this area, current methods perform well enough to be of great value in information extraction. One particularly important application of entity linking methods is that they serve to *disambiguate* mentions to entities [Cucerzan, 2007] in the text (such

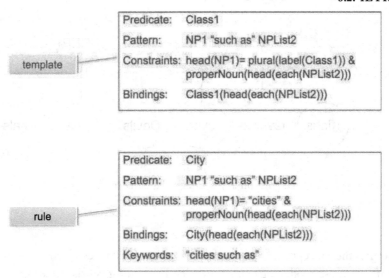

Figure 6.5: Template and rule for entity extraction [Etzioni et al., 2005].

as distinguishing references to President Obama from those to his wife in the example), as well as *cross-document* co-reference resolution (such as identifying all mentions to President Obama in an entire corpus).

Supervised Entity Extraction

Methods such as named entity recognition, disambiguation, and linking often operate without supervision. They are designed to recognize instances of generic classes (e.g., Person, Location, and Organization). As indicated, with the aid of domain knowledge, one can infer other classes (e.g., President, Athlete, and Politician).

There are also methods designed to extract instances of specific classes, for example, by using a search engine to expand a list of known entities. Wang and Cohen [2008] describe an iterative system that starts from a list of seed entities of a given class and, through repeated calls to a search engine, is able to find many more instances of the same class. The method can be bootstrapped as well, exploiting user-provided and system-generated seeds. The authors study various ways of scoring the extraction patterns and tuning the method, achieving accuracy levels as high as 97%. This method employs a single source, namely a document collection, and a single extraction technique. Often we have access to multiple sources (e.g., a document collection, a local database, and the web). Pennacchiotti and Pantel [2009] propose a method that aggregates multiple extractors from different sources, thus obtaining more instances.

A more sophisticated method that combines machine learning with extraction templates, which can be viewed as generalizations of Hearst patterns, is described by Etzioni et al. [2005]. The

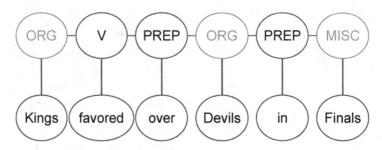

Figure 6.6: Named entity recognition as a sequence labeling task.

starting point is the concept of interest and a known list of instances. Each template is instantiated for the concept of interest, producing extraction rules. Each rule gives rise to search engine queries using the given known instances. Each query is submitted, and the results are analyzed, again through the application of the patterns to extract new instances. Figure 6.5 shows a template and its instantiation for extracting instances of the concept "City." This extraction process continues in a feedback loop: as more instances are extracted, each rule is evaluated to assess the quality of the instances it derives (by comparing a list of known instances) and the number of new instances discovered (by comparing to the list of recent extractions). Once the number of new and high quality instances decreases below a given threshold, the system stops.

Named Entity Recognition as Sequence Labeling

The systems described above rely on fairly shallow NLP techniques, basically on the application of Hearst patterns. Other approaches rely on deeper analysis. For example, the Stanford NER [Finkel et al., 2005] uses both local and global information to detect entities in the text. It is pre-trained against a corpus of news articles to assign PER, ORG, LOC, and MISC tags to entities, as well as mentions to time (e.g., dates) and numbers in the text. The features used for its learning include POS tags, the previous and following words, and also n-grams that capture word dependencies. The method employed here is very similar to that of sequence labeling described above, with the main difference being that now the training data are used to identify entities. Figure 6.6 shows an example of a labeled sequence from a sentence. This approach has a clear advantage of working offline, and also working independently for each sentence (or document). Similar named entity recognition tools exist within all major NLP toolkits.

6.2.3   ONTOLOGY LEARNING

Identifying named entities and grouping them into concepts is often only part of the IE task. A problem results from the fact that concepts are often naturally modeled as hierarchies:

$$person \supseteq author$$
$$book \supseteq children's\ book$$

However, when we extract instances from unstructured content, we rarely know exactly to which level of the hierarchy they belong (as expressed in the corpus). As an example, suppose we are interested in finding professional athletes, together with the countries in which they were born, from documents on the web. Even though there are many documents online referring to Swiss tennis player Roger Federer, his celebrity status makes it much more likely to find documents describing him as a top tennis player or an important Swiss personality, rather than as an athlete. Therefore, if an IE system aims to find instances of athletes, it may be problematic to identify Mr. Federer as such, without using an inference rule stating that every tennis player is an athlete.

More generally, the problem exemplified above is a conceptual mismatch between the classes used in the text and those expected by the IE system designer. It is also important to arrange the classes extracted from the text into a hierarchy expressing the sub-class relationship among them. Such hierarchies are useful in other tasks as well (e.g., clustering and relation extraction), especially in combination with reference hierarchies such as Wordnet [Miller, 1995]. For these reasons, the problem has received considerable attention and remains an important challenge.

Some of the techniques build on methods for instance extraction, such as the iterative application of Hearst patterns to infer a hierarchy of concepts from the text. Snow et al. [2005] use a classifier to discover new instances in unseen text. As compared to the syntactic features of the Hearst patterns, their use of parsing provides more reliable features, including part of speech tags and structural dependencies. To obtain training data, they match sentences that contain nouns with hypernyms already identified in Wordnet. The experimental evaluation, using a corpus of over six million news articles, shows that the resulting concept hierarchy is much more precise and detailed than Wordnet.

Kozareva and Hovy [2010] further extend the ideas to derive a complete hierarchy from the text. The method consists of two steps. First, they repeatedly apply extraction patterns in pairs that are connected by known examples. We start from knowing that lions are animals, and ask for further examples; we then use a pair of animals to find a concept that includes both.

"animals such as lion and ?" → {lion, tiger, jaguar}

"? such as lion and tiger" → feline

The step above determines that feline is a sub-concept of animal (which was previously unknown from the starting facts). The process can be repeated now with feline, this time first finding a concept that includes feline and then finding other examples of that concept:

"? such as feline" → "Big Predatory Mammals"

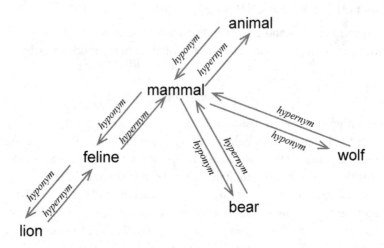

Figure 6.7: Partial class hierarchy extracted using Hearst patterns.

"mammals such as felines and ?" → {felines, bears, wolves}

Now a new concept (mammal) has been discovered. (Typically concepts are named using nouns and do not include adjectives.) The second step in the process is minimizing the number of edges in the hierarchy. This is achieved by removing redundant edges and edges that correspond to paths (e.g., feline → animal is removed once feline → mammal → animal is discovered). The result is shown in Figure 6.7.

The resulting class hierarchy will be determined by what is in the text corpus, and it is possible that mistakes or omissions will occur. For example, in Figure 6.7, it might be best to include a class for *canids*, grouping bears and wolves. However, it has been shown that it is possible to obtain very accurate class hierarchies in this way [Snow et al., 2005]. Nevertheless, there is often a mismatch between the concept hierarchy expressed in the unstructured corpus and that in the mind of the BI analyst extracting data. This can sometimes be resolved by applying the techniques to larger text collections, or manually, by the application designer.

6.2.4   RELATION EXTRACTION

As well as recognizing entities named in a text, BI relies on the ability to find relations between those entities. This problem is more difficult than NER because of several reasons. The first is that the success of relation extraction is highly dependent on the success of NER: small error rates in NER can be magnified when attempting to extract relations. Secondly, a term in the text can denote either a concept or a relation (e.g., author), depending on the corpus and the context. In addition, there are multiple relations among the same pair of concepts, requiring more effort to identify and

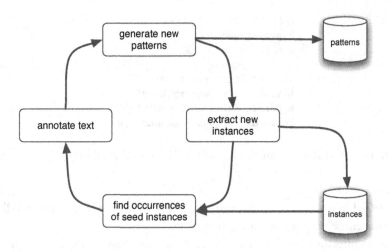

Figure 6.8: Iterative IE extraction cycle.

name the relationships correctly:

$$\text{editor-of-book} \subseteq \text{book} \times \text{person}$$
$$\text{author-of-book} \subseteq \text{book} \times \text{person}$$

As with entity discovery, methods for relation extraction can be divided into closed-domain and open-domain. For closed-domain relation extraction, the goal is finding pairs[2] of entities that are related through a specific relation of interest. Alternatively, open-domain relation extraction attempts to identify all relationships that are described among named entities.

Many methods for closed-domain relation extraction have addressed the problem as a binary sentence classification problem: does the input sentence express the relation of interest (YES/NO). These methods typically rely on deep NLP techniques, such as dependency parsing. Culotta and Sorensen [2004] use dependency parsing tree kernels on a Support Vector Machine to find sentences containing relations. The approach of Bunescu and Mooney [2005] is to consider the distance (in the dependency tree) between the entities that are the arguments of the relation.

Iterative IE Cycle

Before continuing with the discussion of relation extraction systems it is worth pausing briefly to discuss a general IE strategy, adopted in fact by many such systems, which consists of continuously applying extraction tools to gather new information, while detecting new patterns in the process (Figure 6.8). The cycle starts with an initial list of *seed facts* (which could be entities, classes, or relations) and a known list of patterns. The seed facts are first matched in the text corpus; if any

---

[2]Recall that *n*-ary relation extraction can be achieved in a post-processing step, during which multiple binary relations are integrated.

```
Extraction Rule:
NP₁ ''born in'' NP₂
& properNoun(NP₁)
& properNoun(NP₂)
=>
instanceOf(Person,head(NP₁))
& instanceOf(Country,head(NP₂))
& bornIn(head(NP₁),head(NP₂))
keywords: ''countries such as''
```

Figure 6.9: Relation extraction rule in KnowItAll [Etzioni et al., 2004].

fact is expressed in a previously unknown way, a new pattern is then learned. All patterns are then applied to the entire corpus, generating new facts.

This architecture has become prevalent among several existing large-scale IE systems [Agichtein and Gravano, 2000, Etzioni et al., 2004, Paşca et al., 2006, Ravi and Paşca, 2008]. Moreover, this cycle has been adapted in many ways, and used by many production systems. One example is in obtaining training data for improving extractors [Mansuri and Sarawagi, 2006, McCallum, 2005, Wu et al., 2008].

Snowball [Agichtein and Gravano, 2000] was among the first systems for large-scale extraction of binary relations from text. Using bootstrapping, it takes an initial set of seed relations (i.e., known pairs of associated entities), searches the corpus for sentences where these entities appear in close proximity, learns textual patterns from these sentences, and searches the corpus again using these patterns to extract new instances of the relation (recall Figure 6.8). The use of textual patterns in Snowball is akin to the use of Hearst patterns for entity discovery.

KnowItAll [Etzioni et al., 2004] extends NER as shown in Figure 6.5 to discovering relations as well (Figure 6.9). Observe that the extraction of a relation implies the extraction of the associated entities. In order to maintain a reasonable level of accuracy, KnowItAll introduces the use of *pointwise mutual information* (*PMI*) to assess how plausible each extraction is. PMI is a statistical measure, computed across the entire collection, meant to eliminate spurious extractions resulting from mistakes in the algorithm. Observe also that the text pattern specifying the relation is part of the rule. Paşca et al. [2006] propose a system based on the same ideas, but focused on a single "hidden" relation, specified by enumerating its instances, such as (Athens, Greece). The goal of the system is to find other pairs of instances that are related by any of the ways (i.e., any of the patterns) that connect the associated entities.

The systems described so far can be labelled as "one-sentence-at-a-time," as they rely on applying extraction patterns to each sentence in the corpus in isolation. This approach is embarrassingly parallel, since each sentence is processed independently, which leads to high scalability.

Frequency	Pattern	Example
38%	E_1 Verb E_2	X established Y
23%	E_1 NP Prep E_2	X settlement with Y
16%	E_1 Verb Prep E_2	X moved to Y
9%	E_1 Verb to Verb E_2	X plans to acquire Y

Figure 6.10: Patterns expressing verb-based relations.

Open Relation Extraction Using Textual Patterns

The "one-sentence-at-a-time" framework has been extended to the open domain, where the system is not given the list of relations of interest to start with. The task is then finding both the entities and whatever relations exist between them.

Fader et al. [2011] describe open domain relation extraction operating on individual sentences independently. The system improves and refines the techniques described above, using several observations from experience. For instance, the system relies on state-of-the-art Named Entity Recognition instead of assuming entities are simply noun phrases. Moreover, the extraction patterns are defined over POS tags, obtained through text segmentation using CRFs. One striking observation is the rather limited number of patterns that are useful in relation extraction. The authors indicate that over 95% of all relations that can be extracted from text follow a small number (9) of patterns. The most common pattern, responsible for 38% of all extractions, is simply E_1 Verb E_2, where E_1 and E_2 are named entities (e.g., "E_1 founded E_2"). Figure 6.10 shows examples of such patterns.

Relation Extraction Via Text Clustering

An alternative to the "one-sentence-at-a-time" approach has been proposed by Hasegawa et al. [2004], who use text clustering to extract relations among entities. The approach is to build triples $t = \langle E_1, C, E_2 \rangle$ where E_1 and E_2 are named entities, and C consists of text features extracted from all sentences in the corpus that mention the two entities together. The original approach performs the clustering based on the context vector only. Thus, if two triples t_i, t_j appear in the same cluster, the entities in t_i and the entities in t_j are assumed to belong to the same relation. Extracting the label of the relation can be done by inspecting the centroids of the clusters, for instance by using the heaviest features in their context vectors. Both unigrams and bi-grams can be used as features.

Merhav et al. [2012] adapted the clustering idea for large-scale relation extraction over web documents, and compared kinds of features, including unigrams, bi-grams, and features extracted using the patterns of the previous "one-sentence-at-a-time" approach. They tune the clustering algorithm by matching the extractions it produces against the Freebase online database. The original clustering algorithm was modified to take contextual information into account, making it more robust. For instance, knowledge about the entity types was used to modify the weights of the features;

thus, "mayor" would have its weight increased for clustering triples involving a person and a location and decreased for triples involving two persons. This change, alone, led to 12% improvement over the original system.

The obvious downsides of the clustering approach are that it produces a single relation for each entity pair, and it needs to gather a large number of triples before the clustering can be performed. On the other hand, a clustering analysis based on purity reveals that the clustering approach produces fewer and much more concise relations than when sentences are treated in isolation [Merhav et al., 2012]. The brittleness of the "one-sentence-at-a-time" approach, that it cannot identify synonyms, for instance, has been addressed in a rather similar way by using a global algorithm akin to clustering [Yates and Etzioni, 2007].

Higher-order Relations

Most relation extraction systems focus on binary relations. This approach is good for immutable and independent facts, such as a person's birthday, but does not capture the nuances of ephemeral facts (e.g., the host of the olympic games) or of facts that require contextual information (e.g., total sales for a large company requires at least a time period and a geographic boundary).

Zhang et al. [2008] develop techniques to identify the temporal validity of facts. They employ a deep grammatical parser [Suchanek et al., 2006] to locate prepositions that indicate time constraints on the facts. To cope with the uncertainty of the task, the start and end times are represented by intervals. The authors also extract document annotations to identify publication dates, enabling the grounding of references such as "last month."

Wick et al. [2006] propose a task that they called *record extraction*. The goal is to group related entities found in documents into records. This allows, for example, the composition of a contact database from personal web pages. The authors employ the notion of field compatibility to cluster the entities. The field compatibility features are domain specific and have to be provided by the user. The system is trained to learn the parameters that highlight the most relevant features.

6.2.5   FACTOID EXTRACTION

Some IE systems can be categorized as *factoid* extraction tools, aimed at gathering small pieces of information. For example, Kylin [Wu et al., 2008] exploits Wikipedia articles as input to bootstrap IE. The goal is to augment incomplete infoboxes (summary tables containing attributes of the page's subject) with information extracted from text within the articles. Kylin starts by building a concept hierarchy for Wikipedia subjects and finding commonalities among the instances to determine relevant attributes that are missing in other articles. The extractor is trained on Wikipedia articles that mention attributes present in its completed infoboxes, and it is then used to extract values from pages that do not have the equivalent infobox attribute. The proposed system relies on the assumption that attribute values present in the infoboxes are mentioned in the text of the article, which is often true: in fact, most of the information in the infoboxes tends to appear in the first paragraph of the articles. This, of course, precludes the applicability of the technique to non-encyclopedic corpora.

TextRunner [Banko et al., 2007] employs an unsupervised learner to classify its own training data, based on linguistic knowledge. The authors apply a deep parser to a small sample of the corpus, identifying target tuples based on heuristics for the generated syntax tree. The tuples extracted in the first step become the training data that are then used to train a Naive Bayes classifier. The classifier, more efficient than a parser-based approach, is used to extract instances from the entire corpus. Like KnowItAll [Etzioni et al., 2004] and other statistical learning systems, the extracted facts are associated with probability values that reflect their support in the corpus.

Most fact extraction systems focus on extracting facts explicitly mentioned in the text. Culotta et al. [2006] go one step further, analyzing the relational paths formed between the entities. This analysis enables the discovery of implicit facts in the text, for example, the fact "cousin of" can be inferred whenever the relational path "parent-sibling-child" is found to be true between two entities. These relations might also reveal trends such as the fact that children are likely to attend the same college as their parents. The authors use this relational information to improve the extraction process, adding the relation paths as features in the training of their CRF-based extractor.

6.3   DATA EXTRACTION FROM THE WEB

The previous section covered the text-understanding techniques that have been developed by the NLP community. In contrast, this one focuses on the *data scraping* approaches that have been developed primarily by researchers in the database community and rely on syntactic and structural clues present in text markup.

6.3.1   WRAPPER INDUCTION

The advance of the web has allowed research on IE to exploit more structured documents, especially web pages [Chang et al., 2006]. IE from web pages relies on syntactic patterns or layout structures of the documents that repeat either within a document or across several documents hosted at a single site. In this context, the programs that perform the IE task are referred to as *wrappers*, and their job is to enfold information sources, filtering and integrating the data used in the BI application.

Wrappers are based on sets of extraction rules to match and retrieve the desired information. Many wrapper generation systems allow users to specify extraction rules based on a declarative language. However, the structure of documents on the web is complex and contents change periodically, making the specification and maintenance of those rules problematic. To alleviate this burden, researchers have focused on developing systems capable of automatic or semi-automatic wrapper generation.

Semi-automatic wrapper generation systems usually provide an interactive user interface, through which users specify target pages and the information to extract. Based on the user input, the systems create extraction rules and compile the wrapper program. For example, the Lixto system [Baumgartner et al., 2001] uses a datalog-like language, *Elog*, as its internal rule-based language. XWrap [Liu et al., 2000] includes a further debugging step, which follows the extraction process and allows the user to fine tune the rules.

RoadRunner [Crescenzi et al., 2001] addresses data-intensive websites that are generated from a back-end database (as shown in Figure 6.1). This type of website has an even more regular structure, enabling an automatic extraction procedure. RoadRunner iterates over the pages two at a time, refining its extraction rules based on the similarities and dissimilarities. By the end of the process, the repeated fields have been identified and the information extracted. The user, however, still needs to label the fields to make sense of the data.

The accuracy of these methods depends on the quality of the HTML code used by the website administrators, and it has been observed that often this quality is rather low. Nevertheless, the sites remain operational as long as the HTML can be rendered in a comprehensible way to the end users. Based on this idea, some data extraction methods operate at the rendered page level rather than at the HTML level: they render the HTML using an instrumented browser, deriving a Document Object Model (DOM) tree of the content. The extraction algorithm is then applied on the DOM tree instead of the raw HTML code. The DEPTA system [Zhai and Liu, 2005] exemplifies such an approach.

Large Scale Extraction of Tables from the web

Because there is a great quantity of structured data publicly available on the web today, Internet powerhouses have been collecting and cataloging such data. Google's WebTables project [Cafarella et al., 2011] aims at identifying structured data within HTML documents, possibly hidden behind search forms. This system works by analyzing declared tables and lists within the HTML content (i.e., within tags *table*, *ul*, and *ol*). The content extracted this way is analyzed statistically, leading to accurate extraction of attributes (which would correspond to column names in databases or classes in our terminology) and instances. Such data, collected and analyzed in global scale, lead to very accurate discovery of reliable information. The extracted data help at: (1) improving Web search (by exposing hidden web data and adding semantics to the websites), (2) enabling question answering and entity search [Yin et al., 2011], and (3) integrating data from multiple web sources.

6.3.2   SCHEMA EXTRACTION

The typical IE system starts with a fixed schema and the expected output are tuples that comply to the schema. (Even open extraction systems can produce output that conforms to a given schema when only binary relations are sought.) However, information encoded in a corpus of natural language documents is intrinsically unbounded, and having a fixed schema limits extraction to the pre-defined fields. For many applications, it is also unlikely that all relevant attributes can be defined a priori. Some systems have addressed the problem of fixed output.

Cafarella et al. [2007] propose an algorithm for automatic schema discovery from extracted facts. The input for the algorithm is composed of facts extracted by a standard named entity and relation extraction system (e.g., TextRunner [Banko et al., 2007]). The goal of the algorithm is to arrange attributes and values in a set of tables that conform to application-specific parameters. The adjustable parameters encode desirable proportions of the resulting tables (width and height) as well as their attribute value density; for example, a typical data browsing application requires a manageable number of attributes (to fit in the screen) and a high density of attribute values. In the application scenario of the proposal, no prior knowledge about the text corpus is assumed. It is up to the user to analyze and make sense of the resulting unnamed tables.

The approach of Ravi and Paşca [2008] envisages a more focused discovery task, in which the user knows the target class for extraction and agrees to provide some information to bootstrap the process. The input of the system consists of the name of the target class, the target instances (that can be generated by an external automatic process), and a few seed attributes. The objective is to find relevant attributes of the class as well as their respective instance values. Unlike the approach taken by Cafarella et al. [2007], the text corpus is composed of semi-structured web documents and the extraction process is driven by HTML formatting clues in the documents. Attributes are selected based on the similarity of their hierarchical structure pattern (basically, the XML ancestor sequence) and the patterns found in the reference seed attributes.

The extraction process does not need to be unidirectional, always from the input documents toward the extracted tuples. Information from the underlying database can improve accuracy of the extraction process: tuples in the database can help disambiguation during the extraction of new tuples, and the data constraints in the schema can help distinguish correct tuples for extraction. Moreover, existing relational data can be used to generate training data in learning-based approaches.

Mansuri and Sarawagi [2006] exploit clues in the database to augment the CRF extraction model, reducing the dependence on manually labeled training data. The proposed architecture encompasses the extraction and matching processes. For the extraction phase, the authors employ a semi-Markov CRF model [Sarawagi and Cohen, 2004] that defines features over multi-word segments of the text (as opposed to single tokens used in typical CRF models). Sequences are a more natural abstraction for this labeling task, yielding higher accuracy. The authors exploit instances present in the database to derive many features used in the model: word similarity (i.e., whether the word has similar words as attribute values in the database), pattern similarity (e.g., is the capitalization similar to that of the values of an attribute?), and other factors (such as typical length of entities in the database) that are considered together to model an entity classifier. They also extend the Viterbi inference algorithm (typically used in Markov models) to support the cardinality constraints expressed in the schema. Instead of keeping track of the label sequence of maximum probability, the algorithm tracks multiple sequences since now any sequence that conflicts with the cardinality constraints must be discarded.

For the matching phase, the authors design a CRF classifier based on multiple string similarity measures. Variations of the same entity (e.g., J. Ullman and Jeffrey Ullman) are preserved, with the different occurrences linking to a canonical version. The matching model also leverages the relational constraints so that the matching of a given record takes into account associated records from other tables.

6.4   BI OVER RAW TEXT

Most of the methods discussed in this chapter take the stance that relevant BI information is extracted from the text to populate a knowledge base or structured database for further processing. This section briefly discusses another approach, which is to deploy the BI tools directly over text documents, bypassing the explicit extraction of information from the documents. Jain et al. [2008] enable *online processing* of simple SQL queries (selection-projection-join) over the text database. The relations are pre-defined but the tuples are extracted on demand, based on the query. The system optimizes query executions, selecting good document retrieval and extraction techniques.

In most IE tasks, the target schema is fixed, specified as input. Some systems require further input to guide the extraction process. The system proposed by Mansuri and Sarawagi [2006] has no fixed schema. Instead, the user indicates a target database, complete with schema, constraints, and data. The contents of the database are used throughout the extraction process, complementing training data, defining constraints, and aiding data cleaning.

Users can also be more involved in the extraction process. Chu et al. [2007] face the extraction as an incremental and interactive process where the system and users cooperate in discovering the structure hidden in a text corpus. The authors propose a relational workbench consisting of three operations: extract, integrate, and cluster, whose specific algorithms must be chosen by the data administrator on a convenience basis. The schema evolves as a result of the execution and analysis of these operations. In the proposed scenario, a new text corpus is stored in a table, one row per document, and users can issue keyword-based queries straightaway. New attributes are then discovered by the extract operator, the attributes are correlated by the integration operation, and common properties among documents are derived from the cluster operation. There is no specific order for the execution of the operators, and the structures discovered can be either reflected in the table or fed as input to another operator. The authors employ a special table structure, meant to support the high degree of sparseness of attribute values.

Ipeirotis et al. [2006] analyze three different text-centric tasks, including information extraction, together with the available strategies to tackle their document selection phase. The goal is to propose a unifying cost-based optimization scheme. Four document selection strategies are considered: (i) scan; (ii) filtered scan, which uses a classifier to determine useful documents; (iii) iterative set expansion, which uses pre-defined seed tokens to find useful documents, deriving new tokens for subsequent iterations; and (iv) automatic query generation, which extracts rules from a trained classifier to construct queries that return potentially useful documents. The authors define a cost model that covers the four strategies, which enables the selection of an efficient plan based on a given target recall.

Jain et al. [2008] advance that in two main aspects: (i) considering multiple extraction systems to be chosen by the optimizer, and (ii) enabling *online processing* of simple SQL queries over the text database. Online processing changes the traditional workflow of information extraction, where the entire corpus must be processed to extract all relations before any query can be issued. The proposed approach avoids processing and extracting tuples that may never be used, and enables more efficient monitoring of entities in an evolving corpus. The framework also considers data cleaning of the extracted tuples. To account for a user's quality requirements, instead of fixing a target recall, the user must define a *goodness* value that captures the intended balance between efficiency and recall. The main problem in this scenario is to estimate the statistics needed for query optimization. Experiments show that the heuristics proposed in the paper provide good estimates for query optimization.

6.5 CONCLUSIONS

This chapter is not a survey of IE theory or techniques; for that, the reader is referred to Sarawagi [2008] and Nadeau and Sekine [2007]. Chang et al. [2006] provide a good survey of techniques for extracting semi-structured data from websites.

Our goal here is to provide a broad overview of current techniques and ongoing research areas in the use of IE to help in the BI life cycle. There are many other aspects to the problem, however, which are not covered here. For example, text processing tools are very different than traditional database management systems, and such architectural mismatches often lead to performance problems. The book by Inmon and Nesavich [2007] offers a more comprehensive and pragmatic overview of the integration of IE and BI, focusing on system issues, meta-data management, and the integration of other unstructured sources of information (e.g., spreadsheets).

Historical Perspective

The Message Understanding Conferences (MUCs) were initiated by the US Defense Advanced Research Projects Agency (DARPA) to assess and foster research on the automated analysis of military messages containing textual information [Grishman and Sundheim, 1996]. The conferences started in 1987, and there were seven of them until 1997. The tasks changed from one conference to the next, with topics ranging from military reports of fleet operations to news reports on negotiation of labor disputes.

FASTUS [Appelt et al., 1993] is a typical system from the early days of IE from natural-language text. It employs a nondeterministic finite-state language model and processes text in four phases. In the first phase, trigger words are identified and full names are indexed. The second step recognizes phrases, especially noun and verb groups. These phases are responsible for matching and merging the patterns that fill the templates with the extracted information. FASTUS is a simple and, for its time, effective system. However, it has to be adapted to each intended task, with specific trigger words and patterns.

WHISK [Soderland, 1999] is a more advanced IE system. It employs machine learning techniques to learn the patterns to be extracted from training data. It also guides the training process to minimize the number of tagged documents needed. It works with unstructured and also with semi-structured text. For unstructured text, it produces better results when text is first annotated for syntactics and semantics.

Michelson and Knoblock [2008] overcome the lack of structure by exploiting a pre-defined reference dataset for the application domain. For example, to extract information from personal posts of cars on sale, the authors employ a standard dataset of car models. The source posts are matched against the reference set based on a Support Vector Machine classifier modelled with multiple string similarity features. To constrain the search space, the authors apply blocking techniques on the attributes of the reference set. The tests for matching are then restricted to candidate records in a matching block. After finding a matching record, the tokens in the post are aligned with the tokens of the record. The alignment of tokens drives the extraction process. A simple data cleaning procedure follows the extraction, eliminating misspellings and tokens that only introduce noise.

Machine Reading

There has been a great deal of progress toward *macro*-scale machine reading in recent years, focusing particularly on acquiring encyclopedic knowledge. Two noteworthy projects are YAGO [Hoffart et al., 2013], developed at the Max Planck Institute for Informatics, and NELL [Carlson et al., 2010], from Carnegie Mellon. Both projects have the same goal: adding new facts, concepts, and relations derived from web-scale processing of natural language text to an *existing ontology*. Both projects rely heavily on human supervision, though in different forms: YAGO relies on manually created knowledge engineering rules in the form of domain-specific logical constraints (e.g., that an actor can only receive an award for those parts in movies where the actor was cast), whereas NELL relies on reinforcement provided by the users (e.g., through feedback on the correctness of specific extractions). A third approach to web-scale IE is ReVerb/KnowItAll [Etzioni et al., 2011], developed at the University of Washington. Unlike YAGO and NELL, ReVerb does not rely on an ontology. Instead, it adopts a more syntactic approach where generic patterns (over text annotated with part-of-speech tags) are used to extract facts. All systems above are cyclic in nature, working on a loop where the extractors improve over time as more extractions are made and judged (sometimes through feedback provided by humans, as with NELL).

Another relevant line of work is the extraction of information from structured documents in a specific domain. Friedman et al. [2001] describe a system that applies IE techniques to (the text of) scientific papers in the domain of biology and medicine. Such systems are highly effective in that closed domain, largely because of the availability of rich ontologies. Teregowda et al. [2012] describe a system that parses scientific publications in search for figures and tables, without extracting any information from them, however.

Shallow IE at Web Scale

While traditional NLP-style IE techniques such as those discussed in this chapter remain very successful, a new breed of IE techniques, called *shallow IE*, has emerged in the past few years. Shallow IE has been applied to both the social web and the knowledge web with great success, enabling several noteworthy applications. For example, *Semantic search* is becoming a reality in the form of Google's Knowledge Graph and Microsoft's Entity Cube and Probase. Similarly, *question answering* over web contents has been successfully demonstrated by IBM's Watson system. These applications depend on one or more knowledge bases such as YAGO, which are largely extracted using shallow IE and (bounded) reasoning.

As explained earlier, these shallow techniques do not perform deep linguistic analysis to assign semantics to the text. Instead, shallow IE relies on (1) simple *language patterns* such as Hearst patterns; (2) *pre-existing* data, often partially organized in a knowledge base such as Wikipedia infoboxes [Wu et al., 2008] and HTML tables [Cafarella et al., 2008] on the web; and (3) *redundancy* of information (at Web scale) to reliably extract knowledge.

A recent extensive analysis on a industrial-scale web crawl [Dalvi et al., 2012] highlights the need for sophisticated tools well beyond what shallow IE provides. The main argument is that the diversity with which information is encoded in text is extremely high, and relying exclusively on redundancy is bound to miss many significant and useful information sources. This corroborates the need for active research programs. On the other hand, Christensen et al. [2011] show that shallow IE is extremely cost-effective. In terms of computational cost, deep NLP tools are much slower, often by a factor of over 1,000, while the gap in accuracy is not as dramatic as some fear. Particularly for massive corpora on the web, the lack in accuracy is offset by statistical methods that rely on redundancy, making shallow IE methods very attractive.

CHAPTER 7

Information Visualization for BI

Giuseppe Carenini and Evangelos Milios

7.1 INTRODUCTION

The ultimate goal of BI is to enable effective, informed decisions in a company at all levels. However, making sound decisions is often not just a matter of having access to all the relevant information, but it also requires the decision maker to be able to analyze the available data, get insights, and identify actionable items.

It is widely known that Information Visualization can greatly support data analysis, as our visual system allows us to process large amounts of information in parallel. Furthermore, visualizations are external, observable representations that can vastly extend our memory capacity. As a result, once the data are shown graphically, interesting patterns, trends, and outliers can be much more easily perceived.

Information Visualization is often combined with interactive techniques. Initially the visualizations can provide an overview of the whole dataset and then the user, by direct manipulation, can zoom in or filter the data and get more detailed information on demand [Shneiderman, 1996]. In this way, the user can easily explore, formulate and verify hypotheses, reveal possible cause-effect relationships, and eventually identify actionable items.

In this chapter, we present a critical overview of the prominent role that Information Visualization plays in Business Intelligence, by focusing on how Information Visualization can help business users in making more informed decisions as well as in exploring unstructured, textual information.

7.2 INFORMATION VISUALIZATION FOR DECISION SUPPORT

At the highest level, decision makers in an organization are faced with the following two interconnected decision tasks:

- **Performance Management:** Decision makers need to constantly monitor what is the current state of an organization. Then, given that the organization is in a certain state, they need to explain how it got there, and direct the organization to move to a better state. For instance, it may be the case that a company is losing market shares in India. Looking for an explanation, the CEO may find out that the most likely reason is growing local competition. Then, a possible counteraction might be to launch an aggressive marketing campaign.

- **Preferential Choice:** Given a set of alternatives, decision makers need to decide what is the best option with respect to a set of evaluation criteria. For instance, continuing with the previous example, given the CEO plan, the Marketing Manager needs to decide whether the new marketing campaign should be TV-based, Web-based, or a mix of the two.

In the next two sections, we will explore Information Visualizations that have been proposed to support these two types of decision tasks. We will then conclude the discussion of Information Visualization for Decision Support by presenting a brief overview of recent trends in this area, including the visualization of uncertainty and visualizations to support collaborative data analysis.

7.2.1 INFORMATION VISUALIZATION IN THE PERFORMANCE MANAGEMENT CYCLE: INFORMATION DASHBOARDS

Most companies, as they strive to optimize their performance, loop through the cycle shown in Figure 7.1. This process is called the Performance Management Cycle. In essence, a company starts with step 1, setting up some strategic goals (e.g., to increase its market share in Asia). Then in step 2 a plan to achieve those goals is developed, which may involve refining the goals, setting specific targets, as well as allocating budget. After that, while the plan is under execution, the company's performance with respect to the goals is constantly monitored in step 3. Finally, in step 4, in light of variations between expected and actual performance, corrective actions can be taken, old goals are revised, and new ones are considered. Information visualization is especially critical in the third step of this cycle, in which managers need to carefully monitor the state of their company by analyzing data and performance metrics that are constantly collected (center of the cycle in Figure 7.1). Ideally, a manager should be able to identify at a glance if there is any problem that requires immediate attention, or if there is any opportunity that should be explored. A common solution is to create one or multiple performance dashboards, which are visual displays that, on a single computer screen, aim to provide an integrated, coherent, up-to-date view of the whole company, or of parts of it [Few, 2006].

Many different dashboards can be built depending on several parameters which include, for instance, the purpose of the dashboard (e.g., strategic vs. operational), the data domain (e.g., finance vs. human resources), the span of the data (e.g., Company-wide vs. Department), and many others, as discussed in detail by Few [2006]. However, in this chapter, we will focus our discussion only on properties of a dashboard that are common to most dashboards, independently of their specific function. As running examples, we will refer to the two dashboards shown in Figures 7.2 and 7.3 (originally presented in [Few, 2006]). The first one is intended for a Sale Manager, while the other one was designed for a Chief Information Officer of a company.

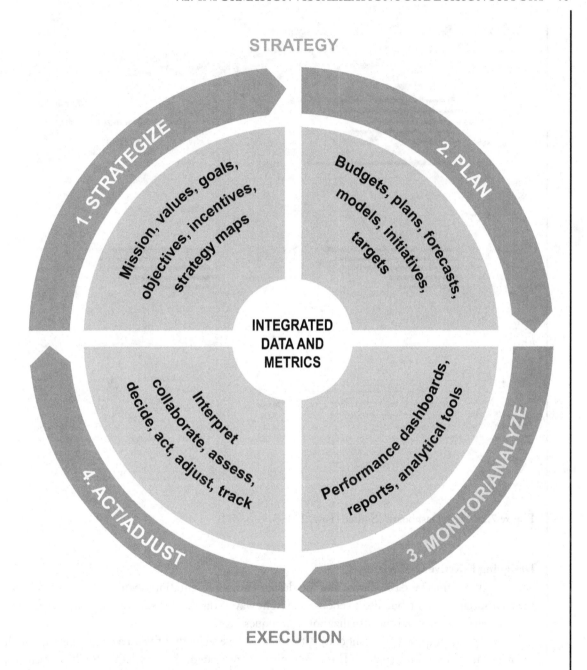

Figure 7.1: The Performance Management Cycle (Source [Eckerson, 2009]).

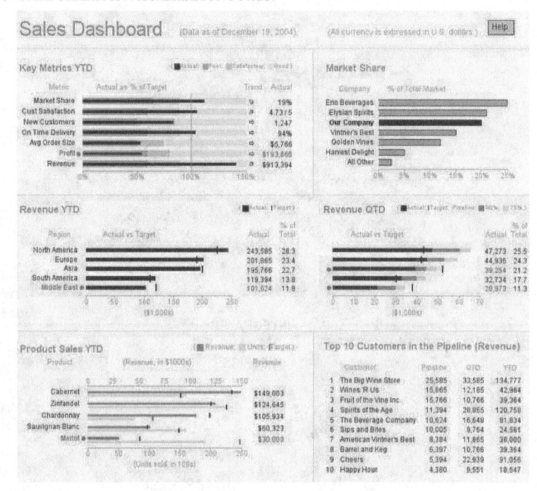

Figure 7.2: Sales Dashboard (Source [Few, 2006]).

Designing Effective Dashboards

The design of effective dashboards, like the design of any presentation, requires not only to select the appropriate content, but also to choose the right way to display the selected content. We discuss content selection first and the visualization techniques next.

Since the purpose of a dashboard is to create an overview that fits on a single screen, not all the relevant data can be displayed. Data are typically aggregated, showing either totals or averages, and when necessary pointing out interesting outliers. For instance, the upper-left panel in Figure 7.2 shows the year-to-date (YTD) total for a set of key performance indicators (KPIs), while the panel right below it shows the YTD revenue aggregated by region. One possible comment (not shown in the figure) pointing out an outlier for this second panel could be something like:"while Middle East revenue is below target, in Saudi Arabia revenue was 30% above target." Choosing the right level of aggregation/abstraction for the information displayed explicitly on a dashboard is arguably the key challenge in designing a dashboard. While it is true that most dashboards allow the user to "drill-down" on the data to access more details on demand, the decision of whether the situation portrayed by the dashboard needs attention and whether it is necessary to drill-down or not is crucially determined by what is shown on the dashboard. If critical information is missing, or it is not sufficiently highlighted, the user will not further inquire the data and will not be able to act on problems and opportunities when they arise. For this reason, the selection of what content should be explicitly shown on the dashboard typically requires an iterative design process, possibly involving a close interaction between a consultant and the end-users.

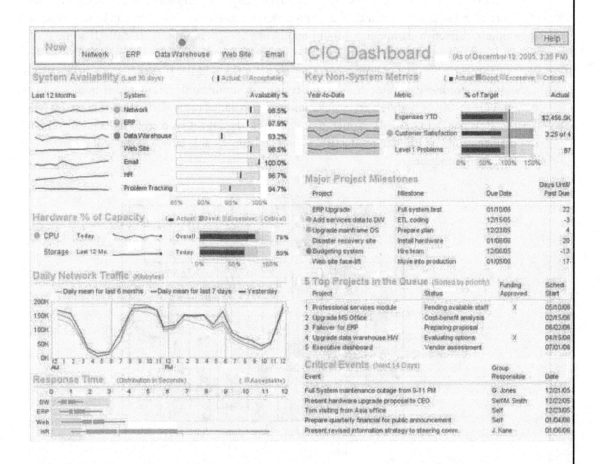

Figure 7.3: CIO Dashboard (Source [Few, 2006]).

Although most dashboards rely on common, easy-to-use visualizations, including bar graphs (Figure 7.2 upper right), stacked bar graphs, line graphs (Figure 7.3–Daily Network Traffic), box plots and scatter plots, there are a couple of novel, but still simple, visualizations that appear to be extremely useful in dashboards. These are bullet graphs and sparklines [Few, 2006]. A bullet graph is a form of bar graph that not only allows you to compare the current value of a performance measure with its target value, but it also allows you to classify current performance with respect to qualitative ranges corresponding to, for instance, poor vs. satisfactory vs. good performance (see for instance the top left panel in Figure 7.2). In contrast, a sparkline is a line graph that is not intended to convey precise readings of the data, but just an overview of what happened in the past to provide context for the current value of a metric. For this reason, they can be very small and have no scale (see the upper-right and upper-left panels in Figure 7.3 for examples).

Several guidelines have been proposed for how the information should be displayed in a dashboard once the content and the visualization techniques are chosen. Even if all the information displayed on a dashboard is critical to decision making, some parts of the data can be more important than others. Effective dashboards should emphasize the more important data. If some data are always more important (e.g., the main KPIs), they should appear more prominently in the layout of the dashboard, either in the upper-left corner or in the middle. If data become important only occasionally. For instance sales in a certain region are significantly below target in a certain time period. This should be highlighted by color and/or by an added colored mark (see Figure 7.2 Middle East in Revenue YTD panel). Notice that changing the layout to convey dynamically changing importance would be counter-productive, as users rely on a stable layout of the dashboard to search for specific information.

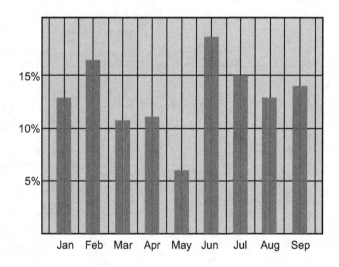

Figure 7.4: Source infovis wiki net.

An aspect of the data that can be effectively conveyed by the layout and explicit graphical connections is when different metrics depend on each other; for instance, when one metric is computed by applying an operation to other metrics, as it would be the case for Net Income being the difference between Net-income-before-Taxes and Taxes, and Net-income-before-Taxes being the difference between Gross Profit and Total Expenses (see Figure 7.5, inspired by Figure 6-5.2 in [Few, 2006]).

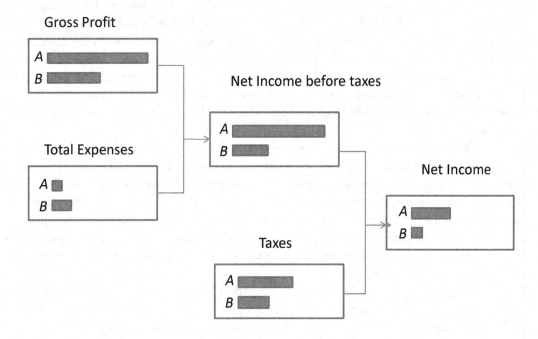

Figure 7.5: Dependencies between metrics are shown by explicit graphical connections.

In most visualizations some of the pixels are used to convey the data, whereas some are providing visual content that does not correspond to data. For instance, in Figure 7.4 the bars are data-pixels, but the grid and the background color are non-data pixels. Effective dashboard should try to minimize the amount of non-data pixels [Few, 2006]. If for any reasons non-data pixels need to be kept, they should be given low visual prominence; for instance the vertical gridlines on a line chart could be displayed in a minimally saturate color (e.g., light grey) as in Figure 7.3–Daily Network Traffic panel. Furthermore, non-data pixels conveying similar structures (e.g., the axis) should be displayed in the same way (i.e., regularized), so that no one would stand out and attract attention.

7.2.2   VISUALIZATION FOR PREFERENTIAL CHOICE

As we have seen in the previous section, a properly designed dashboard should convey at a glance any data points, trends or exceptions that require attention and possibly action. When this happens and the user notices that something interesting and unexpected is happening, she will drill-down into the underlying data repositories to better understand and explain the source of the problem (or opportunity). If this further analysis indicates that action is required, the next step involves deciding what to do. This problem can be often framed as selecting between a set of possible alternatives with respect to a set of criteria. For instance, to continue with our running example, let us assume that a sales manager, while inspecting the dashboard in Figure 7.2, is surprised by the fact that YTD revenues are considerably below target for the Middle East Region. By drilling down, she then realizes that in Saudi Arabia revenues are actually up by 30%, while a big drop in revenues is occurring in all other countries. After further analysis and discussion within her team, it appears that the most likely explanation for Saudi Arabia advantage is that the distributor of their products is a local company they just recently acquired. Now, the group is convinced that they could boost revenues in their biggest market in the Middle East (Kuwait) by also buying a local distributor there. So they are faced with the following decision. Which local distribution company should they buy in Kuwait?

This is a prototypical instance of preferential choice, the decision process in which the best option must be selected out of a set of alternatives. In essence, preferential choice requires consideration of multiple objectives and of trade-offs among them. In our running example, it would be ideal to find a company that is cheap (cost objective), has stores in all the main cities (store coverage objective), and has a well-established track record of sound management (management objective). Yet, in most cases this perfect alternative does not exist, and trade-offs must be considered; for instance between a company with large coverage and average management and one with more limited coverage but excellent management.

A large number of studies have shown that people are generally not very effective at considering trade-offs among objectives, and require support to make this process easier [Clemen, 1996]. Decision analysis has provided considerable help by devising a systematic decision process for preferential choice. The method comprises three distinct interwoven phases. First, the decision maker (DM) builds a quantitative preference model which includes: what objectives are important to her, the degree of importance of each objective (e.g., store coverage may be twice as important as sound management), and her preferences for each objective outcome (e.g., covering all the major cities may be four times more valuable than covering only half of those cities). Secondly, the DM analyzes her preference model as applied to a set of alternatives. The model assigns to each alternative a score, typically between 0 (worst possible) and 1 (best possible). Finally, the DM needs the ability to perform sensitivity analysis in answering "what if" questions, such as "if we make a slight change in one or more aspects of the model, does it effect the optimal decision?" [Clemen, 1996].

Several tools have been developed to support this decision analysis method, and in most of these tools interactive information visualization plays a critical role. A detailed task model for preferential choice, grounded in recent findings from both Decision Analysis and Information Visualization, is presented by Bautista and Carenini [2006]. The model is used to compare analytically a diverse set of visual tools, which include: *AHP Treemaps (TM)* [Asahi et al., 1995], an interface that uses a treemap visualization to inspect preference models; *CommonGIS*

(CGIS) [Andrienko and Andrienko, 2003], a tool for interactive exploration and analysis of geo-referenced data which provides two visualization techniques for visualizing preferences, utility signs, and parallel coordinates; the *Visual Interactive Sensitivity Analysis (VISA)* system [Belton, 2005], a commercial tool for decision analysis, which stresses visual analysis with a special focus on sensitivity analysis techniques; and finally *ValueCharts* [Carenini and Lloyd, 2004], which aims to combine simple visualization and interactive techniques to support the decision maker in analysing her preference model and its application to a set of alternatives.

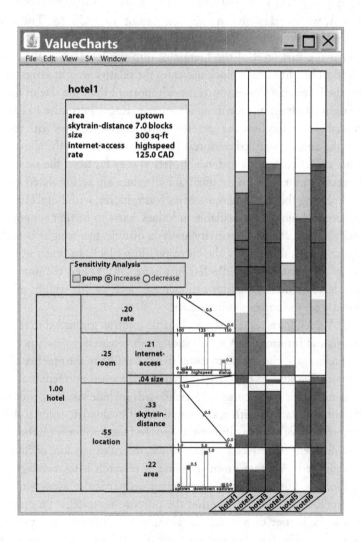

Figure 7.6: Sample value charts.

As ValueCharts are considered to be one of the most promising tools to support the tasks in the task model for preferential choice, we provide a brief introduction to ValueCharts, as an example, by examining its application to the simple preferential choice of selecting an hotel, when traveling to a new city. The reader can find details on the other visual tools in the references mentioned above.

Most people have experienced the decision of selecting an hotel when traveling. You would like to stay within your budget, you prefer the hotel location to be convenient, and you want a room up to your standards. However, often the ideal hotel does not exist, and trade-offs between, for instance, cost, location, and room quality must be considered. A ValueChart for the preferential choice of selecting the best hotel out of six available alternatives is shown in Figure 7.6. For the sake of simplicity, we just describe the key features of ValueCharts. The objectives are arranged hierarchically, and are represented in the bottom left quadrant of the figure, where the hotel quality is decomposed at the first level of the hierarchy, into the location quality, the rate and the room quality. The vertical height of each block indicates the relative weight assigned to the corresponding objective (e.g., the Internet access is much more important than the size of the room). Each column in the bottom right quadrant represents an alternative. Each alternative has a label (e.g., hotel4) and the cell above a label specifies how the corresponding alternative fares with respect to each objective. More precisely, the amount of filled color relative to cell size depicts the alternative's preference value of the particular objective. So, for instance, hotel1 is very far from the skytrain, but it has fast and free Internet access. In the upper right quadrant all values are accumulated and presented as vertical stacked bars, displaying the resulting score of each alternative, with hotel2 being the best alternative. Several interactive techniques are available in ValueCharts to further support the inspection of the preference model. For instance, sensitivity analysis of objective weight is enabled by allowing the user to change the vertical height of the corresponding block. In practice, this can be achieved by using the "pump" function (see middle-left in Figure 7.6). When the pump check-box is selected in the increase/decrease mode, the user can increase/decrease the weight of an objective by simply clicking repeatedly on the corresponding block.

Although ValueCharts represent a reasonable solution grounded in recent findings from both Decision Analysis and Information Visualization, more research is clearly needed to develop effective visual tools for preferential choice and to foster their adoption in the practice of Business Intelligence. One key area for further study is the integration of visual tools for preferential choice with dashboards (see previous section). For instance, should dashboards include visualizations that, like ValueCharts, compare different alternatives with respect to a set of evaluative criteria/objectives? For instance, should the performance of sales in different regions be based not only on the actual revenue, but on a combination of different objectives such as revenue, recent expansion, or future potential expansion appropriately weighted? Another promising line of research is to investigate how different visual tools may be more or less appropriate depending on particular aspects of the given preferential choice; for instance, depending on whether the purpose is strategic vs. operational or on whether the decision is a single user or a group decision, or whether the user performs similar decisions frequently vs. occasionally. Last but not least, most of the data relevant to preferential choice and more generally to Business Intelligence are permeated with uncertainty. For instance, we may only know that revenues in a region have a high probability (95%) to go up, but that is not certain. So, effective techniques to visualize uncertainty would be extremely useful for both preferential choice and dashboards, as we discuss next.

7.2.3 CURRENT AND FUTURE TRENDS IN INFORMATION VISUALIZATION FOR DECISION SUPPORT

Visualizing Uncertainty

As we have already mentioned, many business decisions need to be based on information that is not certain. Uncertainty is common when we assess a value (e.g., customer demographics) because of possible error in the measurements, because of missing data, or because we obtain our values by sampling. When we sample, we only look at a small portion of the population, and any estimate we obtain will come with a confidence interval, which is a measure of uncertainty. Uncertainty is also inevitable when we make prediction about the future (e.g., sales in the next quarter), because what happens in the future is often influenced by highly stochastic and hard-to-predict processes (e.g., weather, people's behavior). Uncertainty can also increase when we transform and aggregate already uncertain data.

Generally speaking, since uncertainty is so common, it is paramount for any decision support system to convey to the user any uncertainty associated with the information relevant to the current decision. And this is especially true for information visualization. While visualizations allow us to process large amounts of data and quickly gain valuable insights, this advantage can be turned against us, if the data is not accurately displayed. In other words, if the uncertainty in the data is not effectively conveyed, the user can quickly reach possibly incorrect conclusions, with an excessive confidence, which is not supported by the data.

A first comprehensive overview of techniques for visualizing uncertainty was presented by Pang et al. [1997]. However, as pointed out by Griethe [2005], most of these techniques were developed for, and eventually applied to, realistic and specialized domains, such as cartography, flow (e.g., wind, current) and volume (e.g., 3D scenes and images) visualization. More recently, there has been a growing interest in visualizing the uncertainty intrinsic in biological data, and researchers have devised more general solutions. For instance, Holzhüter et al. [2012] shows how heat maps can be enriched to display uncertainty associated with microarrays data. Similarly, the visualization of uncertainty has also been investigated in natural language processing. In several applications, including machine translation and speech recognition, while the system computes the set of most likely solutions, it typically only outputs the most likely best-guess. Collins et al. [2007] argue that users of such systems would benefit from seeing the uncertainty inherent in the system output and a novel visualization to convey such an uncertainty as a word lattice is presented.

The visualization of uncertainty for purely abstract information has received much less attention in the literature, with the work of Olston and Mackinlay [2002] being a notable exception. More work in this area is needed to develop standard, robust techniques that can support the visualization of uncertainty on abstract data in BI.

Visualization to Support Collaborative Data Analysis

So far, we have tacitly assumed that in most BI scenarios, although people may use visualizations to collaborate, the actual task of data monitoring and analysis is performed by a single user. However, as datasets grow larger and larger, having a single person to perform a complete analysis of vast amounts of diverse data can become impossible. Furthermore, different people can interpret data differently. Since they may bring to the analysis different backgrounds and information needs, they can come up with different insights and explanations. And a deeper analysis can results from combining different interpretations.

Based on these observations, practitioners have begun to think of data analysis as a more social and collaborative task. Two different types of collaborative data analysis have been studied: asynchronous and synchronous analyses [Few, 2009].

Many-Eyes[1] is probably the most popular platform for asynchronous collaborative data analysis [Viégas et al., 2007]. It provides a collection of visualizations from which the user can select the most appropriate one, for her dataset and intended analysis task. Once the user is done with her analysis, she can upload and share her final visualization and findings. Then, other users can post comments on her work in a forum-like discussion, and create additional analyses of the same data that can complement or contrast the proposed one. Users can also rate existing analyses, which generates a ranking of different displays by popularity. Even if this approach to collaborative visual data analysis is quite recent, its benefits have been already shown in a series of controlled user studies [Heer et al., 2009].

In asynchronous data analysis, like in an email conversation, contributions of different users can be far apart in time or even overlap. In contrast, in synchronous data analysis, like in a face-to-face meeting, users are involved in the analysis at the same time. CoMotion[2] is a well-known framework for synchronous collaborative data analysis. In CoMotion, users can interact within the same visual workspace, and in real time they can explore different aspects of the same dataset and share interesting observations and insights. Synchronous collaboration is especially beneficial when data are rapidly changing and the users may need to quickly revise their conclusions by leveraging the expertise of the other members of the group. So far CoMotion has been successfully applied in sectors as diverse as defense, life sciences, logistics, and homeland security. We expect that, with the growth in volume, velocity, and variety of data in all major industries, platforms like CoMotion will become more and more common for Business Intelligence.

---

[1]http://www-958.ibm.com/s
[2]http://www.gdviz.com/comotionMain.html

7.3   VISUALIZING TEXT

Due to the massive amounts of business-related online and corporate unstructured text accumulating daily, methods that allow its exploitation for business decision making are urgently needed. There have been two main directions that until recently evolved somewhat separately. The first is automatic text mining, which includes key term and named entity extraction, relationship extraction, sentiment analysis and opinion mining, summarization, classification, clustering, and automatic tagging [Aggarwal and Zhai, 2012, Bird et al., 2009, Feldman and Sanger, 2007, Liu, 2012, Manning et al., 2008]. As much of the text generated is interlinked either directly (through hyperlinks), or indirectly (by co-occurring in time or space, through co-authorship, or by virtue of being part of a thread of messages), exploiting the link structure has recently gained prominence. The second direction is text visualization, where modern visualization techniques are developed specifically to allow the user to visualize and manipulate text without any or with minimal text mining as a preprocessing step to extract the text entities that will feed into the visualization. In this section we will survey the state of the art in text visualization, with special emphasis on systems and techniques that attempt or offer potential to cross-fertilize the two directions just described. Examples of text types of relevance to business intelligence include electronic mail, blogs and microblogs, customer reviews, community question-answering forums, the patent, and scientific literature. Text visualization is particularly challenging, as text is discrete data, and therefore it is much harder to map it to images than numeric data.

7.3.1   TEXT CLOUDS

Text clouds represent an early approach to visualizing the contents of a document or document collection. They consist of the set of the most frequent words in the document, which is visually represented as an irregular bubble shape, or a list, containing the words. The size of each word in the cloud is a function of the frequency of the word in the document. Enhancements to the basic word or tag cloud include varying the color intensity to capture recency (in a text stream), as well as grouping together co-occurring tags. When the clouds represent web page metadata, they are called tag clouds [Lohmann et al., 2009].

Tree cloud is the combination of the tag cloud concept with the tree concept, as shown in Figure 7.7. Forming the tree cloud for a document consists of four steps. First, the list of frequent terms is built by preprocessing the text (removing punctuation, grouping synonyms, grouping the different inflected forms of a word, and applying a stop word list). Second, a semantic dissimilarity matrix is built based on co-occurrence data collected over a sliding window through the text [Gambette and Veronis, 2009]. Neighbor joining is used to construct the tree, by joining the nearest neighbors, and rebuilding the dissimilarity matrix based on the joined nodes. Words occupy the leaves of the tree. Color, intensity and size of tags, and thickness and color of edges are used to convey additional information.

Wordle is a variation on the word cloud concept, focusing on the use of color and composition of words, in addition to frequency-dependent size [Viégas et al., 2009]. An example is shown in

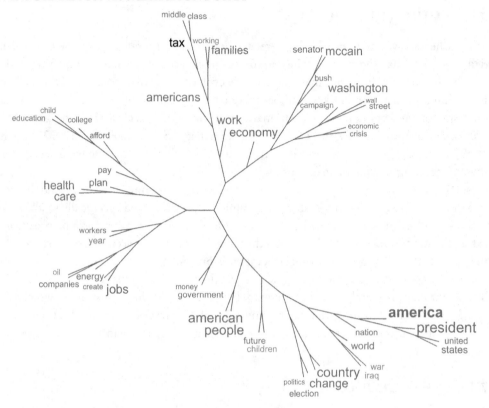

Figure 7.7: 50-word tree cloud of Obama's presidential campaign speeches (Source [Gambette and Veronis, 2009]).

Figure 7.8. The aim of the algorithm is to apply aesthetic criteria to the creation of the layout of the cloud, by varying the angle of words, their order, and the shape of the cloud. Word positioning is based on a greedy algorithm to avoid word overlap along a spiral path.

Word clouds have been combined with other visualization techniques, serving as components of more complex visualizations. Word clouds have been combined with parallel coordinates, to form *parallel tag clouds* [Collins et al., 2009]. In parallel tag clouds, words are arranged in alphabetical order into parallel columns. Font size is used to convey importance of words. Words that are present across columns are connected by edges. Edges have varying width, intended to represent relative size differences among columns. To reduce clutter, edges are shown as stubs, being transparent in the space between columns, unless the user hovers with the mouse near them, in which case they are fully drawn. This feature supports interactive exploration of the data. Additional features of the system include: coordinated views (between terms and the documents that contain them), facets, filtering by selecting columns of interest, and document viewing as full text and tag cloud by clicking

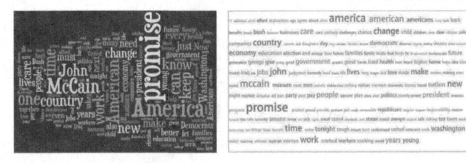

Figure 7.8: Wordle vs. tag cloud of Barack Obama's speech at the Democratic Convention in 2008 (Source [Viégas et al., 2009]).

on a document glyph. An example of a parallel tag cloud, with a variation on the visual encoding to represent both significantly high (red) and significantly low (black) scores is shown in Figure 7.9. Words turn blue on hover.

Figure 7.9: A parallel tag cloud (Source [Collins et al., 2009]).

Word clouds have been combined with node-link diagrams to represent entities and relationships in documents or document collections, in an approach called *WordBridge* [Kim et al., 2011], see Figure 7.10. The data model is based on a standard graph structure $G = (V, E)$, where vertices in V represent entities (e.g., authors, characters) and edges in E represent relationships between entities. Both nodes and edges are associated with a set of keywords, which are visually represented as word clouds attached to nodes and edges in the visualization. The graph is visualized using a force-directed layout algorithm. For word cloud layout, a modified version of the Wordle layout algorithm is used, which is more computationally efficient and deterministic (two invocations of the layout algorithm for the same spatial extent produce the same layout). The user can interact with both the graph layout and the clouds. Nodes can be expanded or collapsed, and clouds can be expanded or contracted by adding or removing keywords (in order of descending or ascending frequency). The WordBridge approach has been used in a web-based visual analytics system called Apropos [Kim et al., 2011].

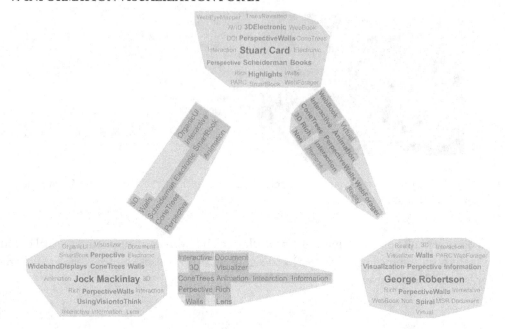

Figure 7.10: WordBridge for three prolific InfoVis authors. Orange clouds represent individual research, while blue clouds represent joint projects (Source [Kim et al., 2011]).

7.3.2 TOPIC MODELS

In text clouds, the typical choice of words to include is based on the bag of words model, i.e., sets of words sorted by an importance criterion (typically a function of word frequency in documents and inverse document frequency in a document collection). The underlying assumption is that word importance represented by frequency captures the topics covered by an individual document or set of documents.

A more sophisticated way of constructing the sets of words to represent documents of a collection relies on topic models. Topic models are generative statistical models of documents. The most widely used topic model is *Latent Dirichlet Allocation (LDA)* [Blei et al., 2003]. Topic models treat a document as a set of words, where each word is generated by a topic (a distribution over a fixed vocabulary of terms). In a heterogeneous document collection, multiple topics are assumed to be present. Given a document collection, described by a vocabulary, and a given number of topics, it is assumed that the collection is generated by a mixture of topics (distributions) over the vocabulary, where the parameters of the distributions are unknown and have to be estimated from the data. The association of a word in a document with a topic is a hidden variable.

Topic models have been used as the basis for interactive exploration of document collections. An author-topic browser for a document collection of computer science publications (a subset of CiteSeer) based on a topic modeling approach has been proposed [Steyvers et al., 2004]. The LDA model has been extended to include authorship information. Each author is assigned a multinomial distribution over topics. The distribution over topics of a document with multiple authors is a mixture of the topic distributions associated with the authors. An author-topic browser has been implemented to support interactive querying of the model. The user can click on one of the topics to view the most likely words for this topic and the most likely authors given a word from this topic. The user can click on a paper to view the probability distribution over topics for the paper. The display is table based (a list of topics, words or authors, and the associated probabilities).

More recently, there has been significant research activity on the visualization and browsing of topic models. An interactive tool for browsing topic models was presented by Gardner et al. [2010]. This visualization presents, in addition to the words describing a topic as a word cloud, the context of the same words (up to 50 characters on either side of a random instance of the word). The user can cycle through contexts to gain a broader view of how the word appears in the text. Furthermore, given a topic, the documents that are most tightly associated with the topic are listed. For visualizing an individual document, its text, the topic distribution of the document, and documents with a similar distribution of topics are shown.

Topic modeling is at the core of TopicNets, a system for interactive visualization of large text corpora [Gretarsson et al., 2012]. In TopicNets, documents and topics are represented as nodes in a weighted graph, with edges connecting documents and their associated topics. The distributions of words given topics $p(w|t)$ and the distributions of topics given documents $p(t|d)$ determine the weights. The system relies on distributed computing and fast inference algorithms to make it possible to learn topic models of large data sets, and sufficiently fast on smaller data sets to permit user interaction. For graph layout, two alternatives are provided: topic-similarity layout and order-preserving layout. In the topic-similarity layout, topics are fixed into position based on a multidimensional scaling algorithm that relies on topic similarity computed from the symmetric Kullback-Leibler divergence between every pair of word topic distribution $p(w|t)$. Then a standard force-directed layout algorithm is applied to place the document nodes in relation to topics. In the order-preserving layout, documents are laid out along the circumference of a circle following a given natural order of the documents, e.g., a timeline.

7.3.3 TEXT STREAMS

Most document collections relevant to business intelligence are in the form of text streams, where each document comes with a time stamp. Visualizing thematic variations over time in document collections is therefore an important problem.

ThemeRiver is an early system for visualizing text streams [Havre et al., 2000], using a "river" metaphor, as shown in Figure 7.11. The horizontal dimension is a timeline, while the vertical dimension is divided into stripes corresponding to different themes. The vertical width of a stripe captures the frequency of the corresponding topic in the collection. Stripes of different themes have different colors. Related themes are assigned to the same color family to facilitate their tracking.

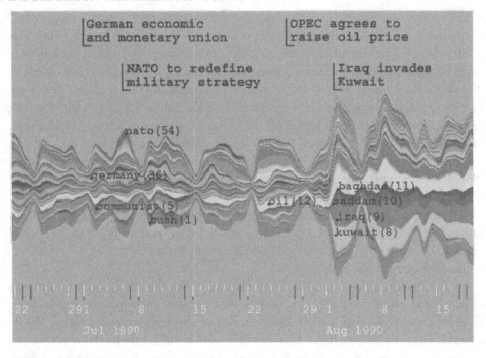

Figure 7.11: Example of a ThemeRiver visualization (Source [Havre et al., 2000]).

CiteSpace is a system for detecting and visualizing trends in the scientific literature [Chen, 2006]. The system takes as input a set of bibliographic records from the web of Science, obtained via a query on a topic of interest. The dynamics of a research field is modeled by a research front and an intellectual base. The research front is defined by emerging thematic trends and surges of new topics, and represented by "hot topic" terms. The intellectual base is defined by groups of articles cited by articles in which terms of the research front are found, and represented by clusters in the co-citation network. Research front terms are identified by a burst-detection algorithm [Kleinberg, 2002]. The co-citation networks over time slices are merged and pathfinder network scaling is used to preserve the most important links. Visualization of the nodes of the co-citation network is in the form of a disk, in which color-coded rings capture the citations in a single time slice. Visualization of the co-citation network takes two forms: research terms as labels of clusters of articles in the network; or as a hybrid network of two interconnected networks, the co-citation network of articles, and a co-occurrence network of research terms.

A more recent tool for visualizing text streams is *TIARA (Text Insight via Automated, Responsive Analysis)* [Liu et al., 2012]. Similar to ThemeRiver, the horizontal axis corresponds to time and the vertical axis to topics and their importance in the form of a stacked graph. Unlike ThemeRiver, TIARA creates much richer visual representations of the topical content as keyword clouds embedded at different time points in the stacked graph (river-like) depiction. The stacking order has been optimized to produce a semantically meaningful and visually pleasing stacked graph. Visual proximity of layers is based on their semantic similarity. Topics and associated keywords were obtained using Latent Dirichlet Allocation (LDA). TIARA offers various interaction tools, including a magic lens (showing names or a network diagram of email senders and receivers under specific topics), and viewing of text snippets matching specific topic keywords. A user study demonstrated that TIARA is more effective than Themail in performing various comprehension tasks on an email collection. It also revealed the importance of identifying entities such as people and events, that TIARA lacked.

Understanding evolving topics in text is the focus of *TextFlow* [Cui et al., 2011]. It extends the concept of stacked graph by visualizing the detailed topic merging and splitting patterns of interest to the users. In addition, it introduces a novel visual primitive called *thread* capturing the emergence and disappearance of a keyword within a topic. The wave bundle and amplitude are visual attributes that capture the co-occurrence interactions between keywords. An example TextFlow visualization is shown in Figure 7.12.

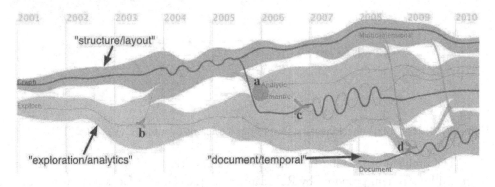

Figure 7.12: The TextFlow visualization of news streams. Topic flows of VisWeek publications related to keywords "graph" and "document" are shown (Source [Cui et al., 2011]).

A novel visualization primitive for visualization of news streams, *TextWheel*, is introduced in [Cui et al., 2012]. It consists of a keyword wheel and a document transportation belt, connected by a dynamic system, as shown in Figure 7.13. Keywords for the keyword wheels are selected according to user interest or as recommended during data preprocessing. The relation between two keywords is encoded by connecting them with a line. Keywords are uniformly positioned around the keyword wheel, while their positions are computed based on their interrelations. The glyph size of keywords changes according to frequency. Documents arrive on the document transportation belt, which has a U-shape. The order of document arrival is based on time by default, but other orders are possible. The speed of document arrival is controlled by the user, who can fast forward, rewind, or even pause the belt to inspect an event of interest. Users can click on a single edge connecting two keyword glyphs, to track the correlation between the keywords over time on a pop-up line chart. Text preprocessing includes named entity recognition, sentiment analysis (Section 7.3.4), and co-occurrence analysis of entity pairs. The significance value of a document at time t is defined as the average of its conditional entropy given its preceding and its succeeding document.

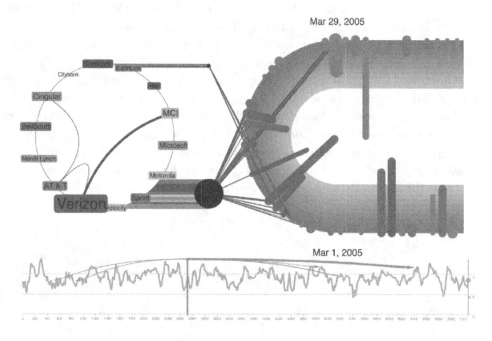

Figure 7.13: The TextWheel visualization of news streams (Source [Cui et al., 2012]).

The problem of tracking the change in meaning (sense) of words in a text stream corpus is addressed by a system proposed by Rohrdantz et al. [2011]. The focus is on words that acquire a new sense over time, or their context is applied to new domains. The *New York Times* annotated corpus (with 1.8M articles from 1987 to 2007) was used aiming to identify words that were given new meaning after the introduction of the Internet. To identify word senses, a context window of 25 words before and after a keyword (ambiguous word) is used, with the associated time stamp. An LDA model is trained on the set of contexts of each keyword, and each context is assigned the most probable topic. The distribution of senses over time is visualized. One view shows the fractions of word contexts belonging to different senses identified by the LDA model. The view for word "to surf" is shown in Figure 7.14.

Email archives are of great interest to business intelligence. *Themail* is a visualization that visually represents relationships based on interaction histories embedded in email archives [Viégas et al., 2006]. Themail exploits the content of messages, as opposed to header information. The interface shows a series of columns of keywords along a timeline. The keywords are extracted from the email messages exchanged between the owner of the mailbox and one other email contact (dyadic relationship). Keywords are separated into yearly words (most frequent over an entire year) and monthly words (most frequent over a month). In terms of user interaction, users can select words from the

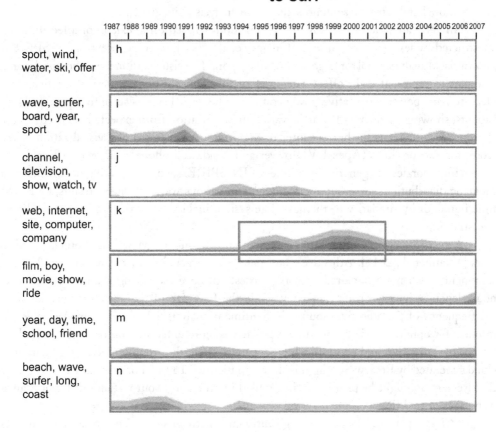

Figure 7.14: Senses of the word "to surf" over time, from [Rohrdantz et al., 2011].

visualization and retrieve the email messages containing them. Words are selected for the visualization based on an adaptation of TFIDF (over month and yearly time frames). Challenges in that system include multiple email addresses for the same person, spam, and forwarded messages that result in artificial repetitions of words, thus inflating their weights.

7.3.4 SENTIMENT ANALYTICS

An important domain of practical interest is sentiment visualization in corpora such as consumer reviews, blogs, or political commentaries. Automatic sentiment analysis or opinion mining of text is a mature area [Pang and Lee, 2008, Tsytsarau and Palpanas, 2012] and constitutes a required preprocessing step for sentiment visualization. Modern sentiment analysis is treated as a Natural Language Processing problem, including topics such as part-of-speech tagging for finding noun-phrases, co-reference resolution, word sense disambiguation, sentiment lexicon generation, detection of conditional and sarcastic sentences, discourse analysis [Liu, 2012].

An early approach to sentiment visualization is based on a lexicon of affect-bearing words constructed by lexical bootstrapping [Gregory et al., 2006], in the context of IN-SPIRE,[3] a well known visual analytics tool for large document corpora. The visualization metaphor used is an adapted rose plot to represent eight affect categories or four concept pairs (positive/negative, virtue/vice, pleasure/pain, power cooperative/power conflict). The rose plot consists of four petal pairs in several variants, showing median and quartile variation or deviation from expected values by drawing the appropriate rose petals further or closer to the origin. An example of a visualization of the affect scores for two products (Apex DVD player and Nokia cell phone) is shown in Figure 7.15. The system incorporates the generic capabilities of IN-SPIRE, such as clustering documents to identify thematic distributions, or grouping documents in various ways (by query results, by metadata, by time frame, or by similarity to themes). The system includes a Lexicon editor to facilitate lexical bootstrapping.

Review Spotlight is a user interface for visualizing online reviews based on tag clouds of word pairs [Yatani et al., 2011]. Adjective-noun pairs are extracted from the reviews, and analyzed for sentiment. Each noun is paired with the closest adjective modifying the noun. Font size of the noun depends linearly on its frequency, while the font size of the adjective depends linearly on the frequency of the adjective-noun pair. Sentiment analysis is based on SentiWordNet, a lexical resource for opinion mining.[4] Sentiment polarity is represented by font color (green, red, and blue for positive, negative, and neutral), while sentiment strength is represented by font darkness. A tag cloud generated by Review Spotlight is shown in Figure 7.16. A laboratory user study demonstrated that Review Spotlight helps users form detailed impressions about restaurants faster than through web pages of traditional online reviews.

LCI is a platform for visualizing sentiment in streams of online social data, such as Twitter [Castellanos et al., 2011]. The system incorporates a sophisticated back end sentiment analyzer which includes the following features: it can learn context-dependent polarity of opinion words; it can handle noisy data sources such as Twitter; it can learn the polarity of non-standard English words such as "liiike" and emoticons; pattern matching rules to detect imperative, interrogative, and declarative sentences, and comparative sentences among the latter based on PoS tags and pattern matching. Opinion is expressed on attributes of entities (e.g., the picture quality of a TV set). Attributes are automatically extracted from the corpus and clustered into semantically cohesive categories, based on semantic distance measured on WordNet. The main visualization element of LCI is the "attribute sentiment cloud" associated with a particular entity or product (e.g., a movie), shown in Figure 7.17. The size of a word in the attribute cloud is determined by its frequency of occurrence, and color indicates sentiment. LCI provides a configurable dashboard with several elements, which include an

---

[3]http://in-spire.pnnl.gov, accessed Feb. 18, 2012.
[4]http://sentiwordnet.isti.cnr.it/, accessed on Feb. 15, 2012.

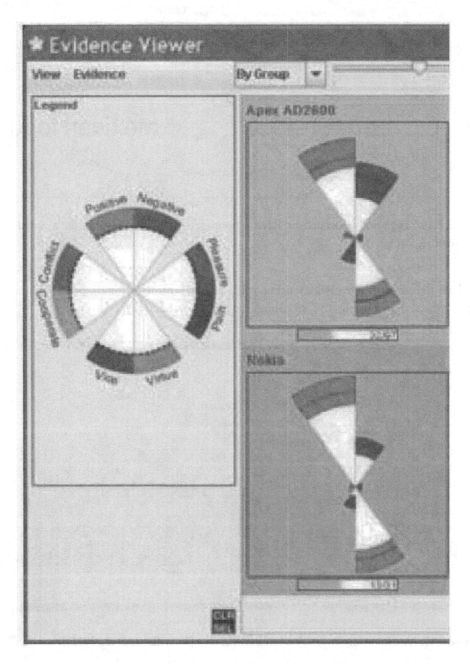

Figure 7.15: Affect visualization using adapted rose plots (Source [Gregory et al., 2006]).

Figure 7.16: Tag cloud generated by Review Spotlight for a set of reviews for a restaurant (Source [Yatani et al., 2011]).

attribute tree, an attribute cloud, sentiment bar charts, sentiment trends, buzz/volume charts, and actual tweets, shown in Figure 7.18 configured for a movie and associated tweets.

Figure 7.17: Attribute sentiment cloud in LCI (Source [Castellanos et al., 2011]).

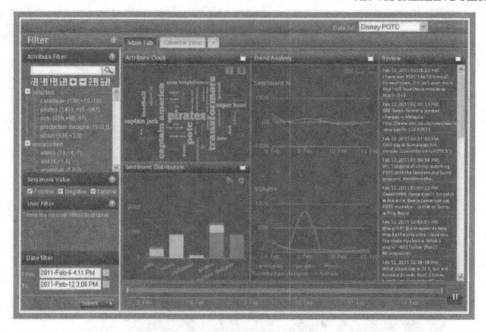

Figure 7.18: The LCI dashboard (Source [Castellanos et al., 2011]).

7.3.5 MULTIVIEW SYSTEMS FOR DOCUMENT COLLECTIONS

In a text visualization system that aims to address a particular practical need a single visualization is typically not sufficient. Multiple coordinated interactive views of the document collection and its contents offer multiple perspectives on the documents and assist the user in making sense of them and in solving associated problems.

IN-SPIRE[5] is a suite of tools for exploratory visualization of the thematic content of large document sets. A text engine behind the visualizations automatically extracts keywords representing topics in the document set based on word frequency and co-occurrence. Each document is then represented by a set of keywords. Similarity of documents based on their keywords allows clustering of documents in a relatively high dimensional space, which is then projected to two dimensions to generate the *Galaxy* and *ThemeView* visualizations. In the Galaxy visualization (Figure 7.19) documents are represented as dots, with short sets of keywords labeling the associated cluster centroids represented as clouds of dots. The ThemeView visualization (Figure 7.20) is a three-dimensional landscape of the document space generated by piling up individual documents, where peaks correspond to dominant themes in the document set, and are labelled by the associated keywords. Peaks in ThemeView are only indirectly correlated with the computed clusters. Additional visual-

[5]http://in-spire.pnnl.gov, accessed Feb. 18, 2012.

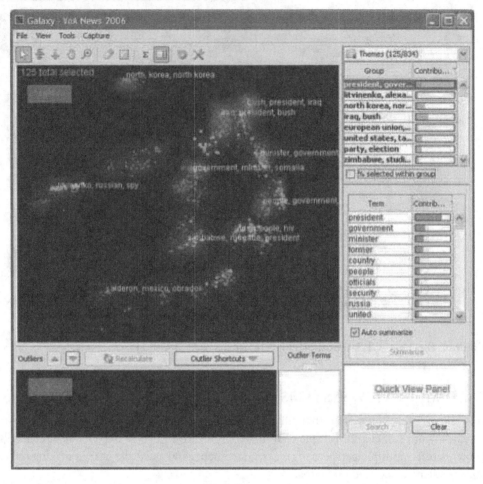

Figure 7.19: The Galaxy visualization in IN-SPIRE.

izations combined with rich opportunities for user interaction for hypothesis formation are included in IN-SPIRE as the following tools:[6]

- *Document viewer* for viewing and annotating individual documents.

- *Summary* and *Probe tools* for identifying frequent terms in documents.

- *Groups tool* for forming document groups and annotating them.

- *Major terms list* for viewing the list of terms used for clustering documents.

- *Searches tool* for searching for keywords by thematic content.

[6]http://in-spire.pnnl.gov/IN-SPIRE_Help5/Content/Overview.htm, accessed Feb. 18, 2012.

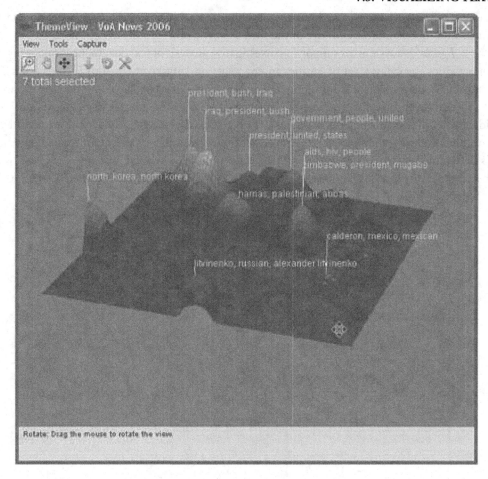

Figure 7.20: The ThemeView visualization in IN-SPIRE.

- *Time tool* for stepping through time-stamped documents.

- *Lexical analysis* for measuring the lexical content of documents.

- *Correlation tool* for examining the relationships between groups.

- *Viewpoints* to tailor visualizations to the user's interests.

The Scalable Reasoning System (SRS) is a descendant of IN-SPIRE [Pike et al., 2009]. SRS is a web-service-based analytic toolkit, which consists of a library of interoperable components, which can be combined to create customized applications. SRS allows the data to be processed by third-party components before it is passed on for visualization. SRS is accessible via a web browser, and because of its web-services architecture, it supports analytics reasoning by a distributed team. It includes a mobile interface for use in the field.

Jigsaw[7] is a system for supporting investigative analysis of text documents, containing evidence of activities involving a set of entities in coordination [Stasko et al., 2007]. Named entities (e.g., individuals, places, organizations, phone numbers, dates, license plates) and their relationships play a central role in investigative analysis, and therefore they are central in the visualization. Entity identification from documents is a necessary preprocessing step. Multiple views are provided, with a focus on displaying the connections between entities across documents. Connection between entities is determined by co-occurrence of entities in documents. There are two types of views, document based and entity based. The *List View* (Figure 7.21) shows connections between sets of entities. The

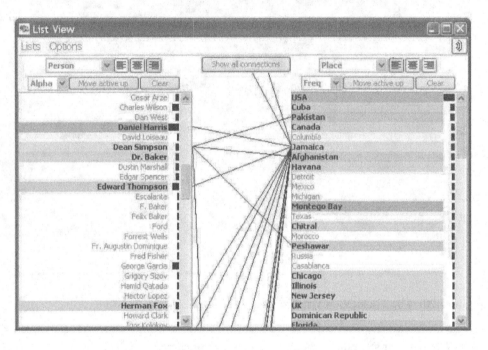

Figure 7.21: The Jigsaw list view.

view contains lists of entity names and their connections. The user can choose which entity types to display and select particular entities, the connections of which are displayed. The *Graph view* (Figure 7.22) displays the connections between reports and entities in the form of a graph. Reports are shown as larger white circles, while entities are smaller circles colored by entity type. The user can select which entities and connections to display, so as not to clutter the display. The *Scatterplot* view (Figure 7.23) depicts pairwise entities between two entity types specified by the user. Each axis corresponds to an entity type, while diamonds in the scatterplot represent reports where the entities

---

[7]http://www.cc.gatech.edu/gvu/ii/jigsaw/, accessed on Feb. 18, 2012.

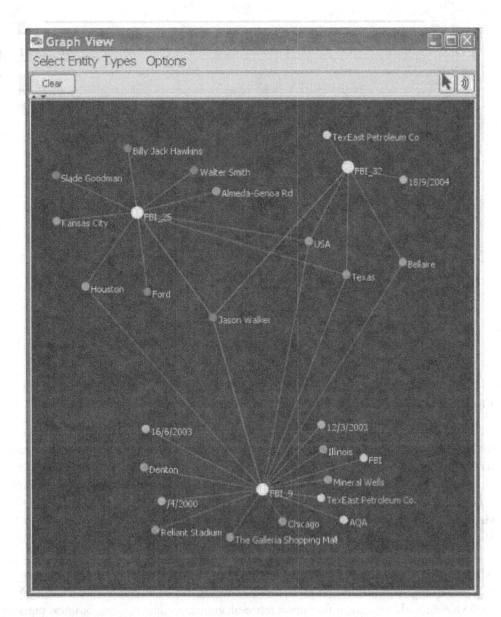

Figure 7.22: The Jigsaw graph view.

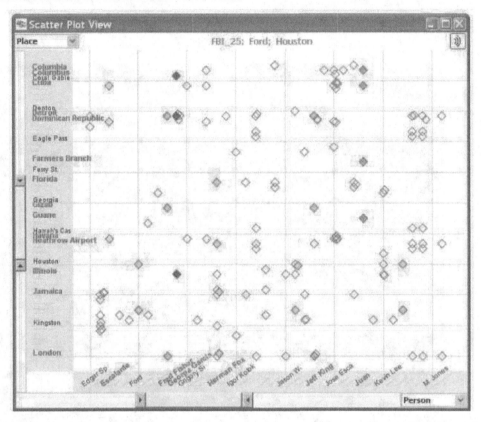

Figure 7.23: The Jigsaw scatterplot view.

in the corresponding x and y positions co-occur. A particular report can be assigned a color so that its multiple instances stand out. Zoom-in is possible on a subset of the entities. A textual report view is also available, in which the entities are highlighted in colors consistent with the graph view. A mouse click on an entity selects the entity for highlighting in the other views. Jigsaw offers additional views, including a Document Cluster view, a Document Grid view, a Calendar view, a WordTree View, a Circular Graph view, and a Shoebox view (to help analysts with developing hypotheses, and organizing evidence). Multiple coordinated views in Jigsaw support opportunistic exploration, where the user picks a point (document or entity) and dives further into it. Jigsaw has been applied to a broad range of domains and tasks, such as investigative analysis of criminal activities, analysis of the biomedical literature, information retrieval, grants, product reviews, business press releases.

Many Eyes from IBM,[8] which we already mentioned in Section 7.2.3, is an experimental platform aimed at making basic visualization techniques available to the general public. Users can

---

[8]http://www-958.ibm.com/, accessed on Feb. 18, 2012.

upload data sets and apply available visualizations on them. The suite of visualization options includes four visualizations for text, Tag Cloud, Word Cloud Generator, Word Tree (a visual version of a suffix tree) and Phrase Net (a hybrid between the tag cloud and word tree) [van Ham et al., 2009]. Users can also upload and make available their own visualization tools.

7.4   CONCLUSIONS

In this chapter, we present an overview of the state of the art in information visualization for business intelligence. Information visualization for decision support of business decision makers assists in the two generic tasks of performance management and preferential choice. Information dashboards are a general approach for business information visualization. Current trends include visualization of uncertainty and visualization to support collaborative data analysis. As business text is becoming a major type of information for business decision making, we reviewed key approaches to text visualization, including text clouds, topic models, text streams, sentiment analytics, and multiview systems which can be viewed as specialized information dashboards for text. An inherent challenge in information visualization for business intelligence is the rigorous evaluation of proposed techniques. User studies have shortcomings because the strength of proposed techniques only becomes evident in large scale, real business settings, which do not lend themselves easily to user studies. Another research frontier is information visualization on mobile devices, where screen real estate is limited and maintaining context for the user as she navigates large information spaces is critical.

Bibliography

Serge Abiteboul, Peter Buneman, and Dan Suciu. *Data on the Web: From Relations to Semistructured Data and XML*. Morgan Kaufmann, 1999. ISBN 1-55860-622-X. 40

S. Abiteboul and O. Duschka. Complexity of answering queries using materialized views. In *Proc. 17th ACM SIGACT-SIGMOD-SIGART Symp. on Principles of Database Systems*, pages 254–263, 1998. DOI: 10.1145/275487.275516 60

Serge Abiteboul, Richard Hull, and Victor Vianu. *Foundations of Databases*. Addison-Wesley, 1995. 41

Serge Abiteboul, Paris C. Kanellakis, and Gösta Grahne. On the representation and querying of sets of possible worlds. *Theor. Comp. Sci.*, 78(1):158–187, 1991. DOI: 10.1016/0304-3975(51)90007-2 41, 43

Foto N. Afrati and Phokion G. Kolaitis. Answering aggregate queries in data exchange. In *Proc. 27th ACM SIGACT-SIGMOD-SIGART Symp. on Principles of Database Systems*, pages 129–138, 2008. DOI: 10.1145/1376916.1376936 43

Charu Aggarwal and ChengXiang Zhai, editors. *Mining Text Data*. Springer, 2012. DOI: 10.1007/978-1-4614-3223-4 105

Eugene Agichtein and Luis Gravano. Snowball: extracting relations from large plain-text collections. In *Proc. 5th ACM Int. Conf. on Digital Libraries*, pages 85–94, 2000. DOI: 10.1145/336597.336644 82

Bogdan Alexe, Laura Chiticariu, Renée J. Miller, and Wang Chiew Tan. Muse: Mapping understanding and design by example. In *Proc. 24th Int. Conf. on Data Engineering*, pages 10–19, 2008a. DOI: 10.1109/ICDE.2008.4497409 44

Bogdan Alexe, Mauricio A. Hernández, Lucian Popa, and Wang Chiew Tan. MapMerge: correlating independent schema mappings. *Proc. VLDB Endowment*, 3(1):81–92, 2010. DOI: 10.1007/s00778-012-0264-z 43

Bogdan Alexe, Wang Chiew Tan, and Yannis Velegrakis. STBenchmark: towards a benchmark for mapping systems. *Proc. VLDB Endowment*, 1(1):230–244, 2008b. 44

Bogdan Alexe, Balder ten Cate, Phokion G. Kolaitis, and Wang Chiew Tan. EIRENE: interactive design and refinement of schema mappings via data examples. *Proc. VLDB Endowment*, 4(12): 1414–1417, 2011c. 44

Bogdan Alexe, Balder ten Cate, Phokion G. Kolaitis, and Wang Chiew Tan. Designing and refining schema mappings via data examples. In *Proc. ACM SIGMOD Int. Conf. on Management of Data*, pages 133–144, 2011a. 44

Bogdan Alexe, Balder ten Cate, Phokion G. Kolaitis, and Wang Chiew Tan. Characterizing schema mappings via data examples. *ACM Trans. Database Syst.*, 36(4):Article 23, 2011b. DOI: 10.1145/1807085.1807120 44

Rema Ananthanarayanan, Vijil Chenthamarakshan, Prasad M Deshpande, and Raghuram Krishnapuram. Rule based synonyms for entity extraction from noisy text. In *Proc. 2nd Workshop on Analytics for Noisy Unstructured Text Data*, pages 31–38, 2008. DOI: 10.1145/1390749.1390756 74

Natalia V. Andrienko and Gennady L. Andrienko. Informed spatial decisions through coordinated views. *Information Visualization*, 2:270–285, 2003. DOI: 10.1057/palgrave.ivs.9500058 101

Apache. Welcome to Apache Hadoop!, 2011. URL http://hadoop.apache.org/common/docs/r0.14.4/. (Last checked December 2012). 15

Douglas E. Appelt, Jerry R. Hobbs, John Bear, David J. Israel, and Mabry Tyson. FASTUS: a finite-state processor for information extraction from real-world text. In *Proc. 13th Int. Joint Conf. on AI*, pages 1172–1178, 1993. 89

Marcelo Arenas, Leopoldo E. Bertossi, and Jan Chomicki. Consistent query answers in inconsistent databases. In *Proc. ACM SIGACT-SIGMOD Symp. on Principles of Database Systems*, pages 68–79, 1999. DOI: 10.1145/303976.303983 44

M. Armbrust, A. Fox, R. Griffith, A. D. Joseph, R. Katz, A. Konwinski, G. Lee, D. Patterson, A. Rabkin, I. Stoica, and M. Zaharia. A view of cloud computing. *Commun. ACM*, 53(4):50–58, April 2010. DOI: 10.1145/1721654.1721672 5

Patricia C. Arocena, Renée J. Miller, and John Mylopoulos. The vivification problem in real-time business intelligence: A vision. In *Enabling Real-Time Business Intelligence – Proc. 6th Int. Workshop*, 2012. 39, 51

Toshiyuki Asahi, David Turo, and Ben Shneiderman. Visual decision-making: Using treemaps for the analytic hierarchy process. In *Proc. SIGCHI Conf. on Human Factors in Computing Systems*, pages 405–406, 1995. DOI: 10.1145/223355.223747 100

Michele Banko, Michael J. Cafarella, Stephen Soderland, Matthew Broadhead, and Oren Etzioni. Open information extraction from the web. In *Proc. 20th Int. Joint Conf. on AI*, pages 2670–2676, 2007. DOI: 10.1145/1409360.1409378 85, 86

Daniele Barone, Lei Jian, Daniel Amyot, and John Mylopoulos. Composite indicators for business intelligence. In *Proc. 30th Int. Conf. on Conceptual Modeling*, pages 448–454, 2011a. DOI: 10.1007/978-3-642-24606-7_35 32

Daniele Barone, Lei Jiang, Daniel Amyot, and John Mylopoulos. Reasoning with key performance indicators. In *The Practice of Enterprise Modeling– Proc. 4th IFIP WG8.1 Working Conf. on the Practice of Enterprise Modeling (PoEM'11)*, pages 82–96, 2011b. DOI: 10.1007/978-3-642-24849-8_7 32

Daniele Barone, John Mylopoulos, Lei Jiang, and Daniel Amyot. Business intelligence model, ver. 1.0. Technical Report CSRG-607, Department of Computer Science, University of Toronto, 2010a. 28

Daniele Barone, Eric S. K. Yu, Jihyun Won, Lei Jiang, and John Mylopoulos. Enterprise modeling for business intelligence. In *The Practice of Enterprise Modeling–Proc. 3rd IFIP WG8.1 Working Conf. on the Practice of Enterprise Modeling*, pages 31–45, 2010b. DOI: 10.1007/978-3-642-16782-9_3 28

Robert Baumgartner, Sergio Flesca, and Georg Gottlob. Visual web information extraction with Lixto. In *Proc. 27th Int. Conf. on Very Large Data Bases*, pages 119–128, 2001. 70, 85

Jeanette Bautista and Giuseppe Carenini. An integrated task-based framework for the design and evaluation of visualizations to support preferential choice. In *Proc. Int. Working Conf. on Advanced Visual Interfaces*, pages 217–224, 2006. DOI: 10.1145/1133265.1133308 100

M.J. Beller and A. Barnett. Next generation business analytics, 2009. (Last checked December 2012). 8

Valerie Belton. VISA: visual interactive sensitivity analysis. SIMUL8 Corporation, Boston, MA, 2005. 101

Omar Benjelloun, Hector Garcia-Molina, David Menestrina, Qi Su, Steven Euijong Whang, and Jennifer Widom. Swoosh: a generic approach to entity resolution. *VLDB J.*, 18(1):255–276, 2009. DOI: 10.1007/s00778-008-0098-x 45

Philip A. Bernstein, Fausto Giunchiglia, Anastasios Kementsietsidis, John Mylopoulos, Luciano Serafini, and Ilya Zaihrayeu. Data management for peer-to-peer computing : A vision. In *Proc. 5th Int. Workshop on the World Wide Web and Databases*, pages 89–94, 2002. 64

L. Bertossi. *Database Repairing and Consistent Query Answering*. Synthesis Lectures on Data Management. Morgan & Claypool, 2011. DOI: 10.2200/S00379ED1V01Y201108DTM020 4

C. Biemann. Ontology learning from text: A survey of methods. *LDV Forum*, 20(2):75–93, 2005. 57

128 BIBLIOGRAPHY

Steven Bird, Ewan Klein, and Edward Loper:. *Natural Language Processing with Python*. O'Reilly Media, Inc., 2009. 105

David M. Blei, Andrew Y. Ng, and Michael I. Jordan. Latent dirichlet allocation. *J. Mach. Learn. Res.*, 3:993–1022, 2003. 108

Jens Bleiholder and Felix Naumann. Declarative data fusion - syntax, semantics, and implementation. In *Proc. 9th East European Conf. Advances in Databases and Information Systems*, pages 58–73, 2005. DOI: 10.1007/11547686_5 45

Jens Bleiholder and Felix Naumann. Conflict handling strategies in an integrated information system. In *Proc. IJCAI Workshop on Information of the Web*, 2006. 46

Jens Bleiholder and Felix Naumann. Data fusion. *ACM Comput. Surv.*, 41(1):Article 1, 2008. DOI: 10.1145/1456650.1456651 45

Kalina Bontcheva, Marin Dimitrov, Diana Maynard, Valentin Tablan, and Hamish Cunningham. Shallow methods for named entity coreference resolution. In *Chaînes de références et résolveurs d'anaphores, Workshop at 9th Annual Conference on Natural Language Processing (le Traitement Automatique des Langues Naturelles)*, 2002. 76

Razvan C. Bunescu and Raymond J. Mooney. A shortest path dependency kernel for relation extraction. In *Proc. Human Language Technology Conf. and 2005 Conf. on Empirical Methods in Natural Language Processing*, pages 724–731, 2005. DOI: 10.3115/1220575.1220666 81

M. Burke and T. Hiltbrand. How gamification will change business intelligence. *Business Intelligence J.*, 16(2):8–16, 2011. 15

Michael J. Cafarella, Alon Halevy, and Jayant Madhavan. Structured data on the web. *Commun. ACM*, 54(2):72–79, 2011. DOI: 10.1145/1897816.1897839 86

Michael J. Cafarella, Alon Halevy, Daisy Zhe Wang, Eugene Wu, and Yang Zhang. WebTables: exploring the power of tables on the web. *Proc. VLDB Endowment*, 1(1):538–549, 2008. 91

Michael J. Cafarella, Dan Suciu, and Oren Etzioni. Navigating extracted data with schema discovery. In *Proc. 10th Int. Workshop on the World Wide Web and Databases*, 2007. 86, 87

Giuseppe Carenini and John Lloyd. Value charts: Analyzing linear models expressing preferences and evaluations. In *Proc. Int. Working Conf. on Advanced Visual Interfaces*, pages 150–157, 2004. DOI: 10.1145/989863.989885 101

G. Carenini, G. Murray, and R. Ng. *Methods for Mining and Summarizing Text Conversations*. Synthesis Lectures on Data Management. Morgan & Claypool, 2011. DOI: 10.2200/S00363ED1V01Y201105DTM017 5

Andrew Carlson, Justin Betteridge, Bryan Kisiel, Burr Settles, Estevam R. Hruschka Jr., and Tom M. Mitchell. Toward an architecture for never-ending language learning. In *Proc. 24th National Conf. on Artificial Intelligence*, 2010. 90

Malu Castellanos, Umeshwar Dayal, Meichun Hsu, Riddhiman Ghosh, Mohamed Dekhil, Yue Lu, Lei Zhang, and Mark Schreiman. LCI: a social channel analysis platform for live customer intelligence. In *Proc. ACM SIGMOD Int. Conf. on Management of Data*, pages 1049–1058, 2011. DOI: 10.1145/1989323.1989436 114, 116, 117

C.-H. Chang, M. Kayed, R. Girgis, and K.F. Shaalan. A survey of web information extraction systems. *IEEE Trans. Knowl. and Data Eng.*, 18(10):1411 –1428, 2006. DOI: 10.1109/TKDE.2006.152 85, 89

Surajit Chaudhuri, Venkatesh Ganti, and Dong Xin. Mining document collections to facilitate accurate approximate entity matching. *Proc. VLDB Endowment*, 2(1):395–406, 2009. 74

Chaomei Chen. CiteSpace II: detecting and visualizing emerging trends and transient patterns in scientific literature. *J. Am. Soc. Inf. Sci. Technol.*, 57:359–377, 2006. DOI: 10.1002/asi.20317 110

H. Chesbrough, W. Vanhaverbeke, and J. West. Open innovation: A new paradigm for understanding industrial innovation. In H. Chesbrough, W. Vanhaverbeke, and J. West, editors, *Open Innovation: Researching a New Paradigm*, pages 1–12. Oxford University Press, 2006. 12

Laura Chiticariu and Wang Chiew Tan. Debugging schema mappings with routes. In *Proc. 32nd Int. Conf. on Very Large Data Bases*, pages 79–90, 2006. 44

Janara Christensen, Mausam, Stephen Soderland, and Oren Etzioni. An analysis of open information extraction based on semantic role labeling. In *Proc. 6th Int. Conf. on Knowledge Capture*, pages 113–120, 2011. DOI: 10.1145/1999676.1999697 91

Eric Chu, Akanksha Baid, Ting Chen, AnHai Doan, and Jeffrey F. Naughton. A relational approach to incrementally extracting and querying structure in unstructured data. In *Proc. 33rd Int. Conf. on Very Large Data Bases*, pages 1045–1056, 2007. 88

Lawrence Chung, Brian A Nixon, Eric Yu, and John Mylopoulos. *Non-Functional Requirements in Software Engineering*. Kluwer Academic Publishers, 2000. DOI: 10.1007/978-1-4615-5269-7 30, 32

Robert T. Clemen. *Making Hard Decisions*. Duxbury Press, 2nd edition, 1996. 100

Christopher Collins, Sheelagh, and Gerald Penn. Visualization of uncertainty in lattices to support decision-making. In *Proc. 9th Joint Eurographics/IEEE VGTC Conf. on Visualization*, pages 51–58, 2007. DOI: 10.2312/VisSym 103

130 BIBLIOGRAPHY

C. Collins, F.B. Viégas, and M. Wattenberg. Parallel tag clouds to explore and analyze faceted text corpora. In *Proc. IEEE Symp. on Visual Analytics Science and Technology*, pages 91–98, 2009. DOI: 10.1109/VAST.2009.5333443 106, 107

Valter Crescenzi, Giansalvatore Mecca, and Paolo Merialdo. Roadrunner: Towards automatic data extraction from large web sites. In *Proc. 27th Int. Conf. on Very Large Data Bases*, pages 109–118, 2001. 86

Silviu Cucerzan. Large-scale named entity disambiguation based on Wikipedia data. In *Proc. 2007 Joint Conf. on Empirical Methods in Natural Language Processing and Computational Natural Language Learning*, pages 708–716, 2007. 76

Weiwei Cui, Shixia Liu, Li Tan, Conglei Shi, Yangqiu Song, Zekai Gao, Huamin Qu, and Xin Tong. Textflow: Towards better understanding of evolving topics in text. *IEEE Trans. Visualization and Comp. Graphics*, 17(12):2412–2421, 2011. DOI: 10.1109/TVCG.2011.239 111

Weiwei Cui, Huamin Qu, Hong Zhou, Wenbin Zhang, and Steve Skiena. Watch the story unfold with textwheel: Visualization of large-scale news streams. *ACM Trans. Intell. Syst. Technol.*, 3(2): 20:1–20:17, 2012. DOI: 10.1145/2089094.2089096 111, 112

Aron Culotta, Andrew McCallum, and Jonathan Betz. Integrating probabilistic extraction models and data mining to discover relations and patterns in text. In *Proc. Conf. on Human Language Technology Conference of the North American Chapter of the Association of Computational Linguistics*, pages 296–303, 2006. DOI: 10.3115/1220835.1220873 85

Aron Culotta and Jeffrey S. Sorensen. Dependency tree kernels for relation extraction. In *Proc. 42nd Annual Meeting Assoc. for Computational Linguistics*, pages 423–429, 2004. 81

Hamish Cunningham, Diana Maynard, Kalina Bontcheva, Valentin Tablan, Niraj Aswani, Ian Roberts, Genevieve Gorrell, Adam Funk, Angus Roberts, Danica Damljanovic, Thomas Heitz, Mark A. Greenwood, Horacio Saggion, Johann Petrak, Yaoyong Li, and Wim Peters. *Text Processing with GATE (Version 6)*. University of Sheffield Department of Computer Science, 2011. 69

Nilesh Dalvi, Ashwin Machanavajjhala, and Bo Pang. An analysis of structured data on the web. *Proc. VLDB Endowment*, 5(7):680–691, 2012. 91

Anne Dardenne, Axel Van Lamsweerde, and Stephen Fickas. Goal-directed requirements acquisition. *Sci. of Comput. Program.*, 20(1-2):3–50, 1993. DOI: 10.1016/0167-6423(93)90021-G 30

Thomas H. Davenport and James E. Short. The new industrial engineering: Information technology and business process redesign. *Sloan Man. Rev.*, 31(4):11–27, 1990. 22

Umeshwar Dayal, Kevin Wilkinson, Alkis Simitsis, and Malu Castellanos. Business processes meet operational business intelligence. *Q. Bull. IEEE TC on Data Eng.*, 32(3):35–41, 2009. 20, 21

Richard T. Dealtry. *Dynamic SWOT Analysis*. Dynamic SWOT Associates, 1994. 28, 29

D. Deutch and T. Milo. *Business Processes: a Database Perspective*. Synthesis Lectures on Data Management. Morgan & Claypool, 2012. DOI: 10.2200/S00430ED1V01Y201206DTM027 4, 32

Jana Diesner and Kathleen M. Carley. Conditional random fields for entity extraction and ontological text coding. *Comput. Math. Organ. Theory*, 14(3):248–262, 2008. DOI: 10.1007/s10588-008-9029-z 73

Denise Draper, Alon Y. Halevy, and Daniel S. Weld. The nimble xml data integration system. In *Proc. 17th Int. Conf. on Data Engineering*, pages 155–160, 2001. DOI: 10.1109/ICDE.2001.914824 65

Oliver M. Duschka and Michael R. Genesereth. Query planning in infomaster. In *Proc. 1997 ACM Symp. on Applied Computing*, pages 109–111, 1997. DOI: 10.1145/331697.331719 58

Wayne Eckerson. The performance management cycle. *Best Practices Report*, 2009. 95

EDM Council. OMG FDTF/EDM Council financial industry business ontology background, 2011. 57

EDN. Program trading averaged 34.1 percent of NYSE during Dec. 27-30, January 06 2012. (Last checked December 2012). 12

Ahmed K. Elmagarmid, Panagiotis G. Ipeirotis, and Vassilios S. Verykios. Duplicate record detection: A survey. *IEEE Trans. Knowl. and Data Eng.*, 19(1):1–16, 2007. DOI: 10.1109/TKDE.2007.250581 45

Oren Etzioni, Michael Cafarella, Doug Downey, Stanley Kok, Ana-Maria Popescu, Tal Shaked, Stephen Soderland, Daniel S. Weld, and Alexander Yates. Web-scale information extraction in knowitall: (preliminary results). In *Proc. 13th Int. World Wide Web Conf.*, pages 100–110, 2004. DOI: 10.1145/988672.988687 72, 82, 85

Oren Etzioni, Michael Cafarella, Doug Downey, Ana-Maria Popescu, Tal Shaked, Stephen Soderland, Daniel S. Weld, and Alexander Yates. Unsupervised named-entity extraction from the web: An experimental study. *Artificial Intel.*, 165(1):91–134, 2005. DOI: 10.1016/j.artint.2005.03.001 77

Oren Etzioni, Anthony Fader, Janara Christensen, Stephen Soderland, and Mausam. Open information extraction: The second generation. In *Proc. 22nd Int. Joint Conf. on AI*, pages 3–10, 2011. DOI: 10.5591/978-1-57735-516-8/IJCAI11-012 90

B. Evelson. Topic overview: business intelligence. Technical report, Forrester Research, 2008. (Last checked December 2012). 8

Anthony Fader, Michael Schmitz, Robert Bart, Stephen Soderland, and Oren Etzioni. Identifying relations for open information extraction. In *Proc. 2011 Conf. on Empirical Methods in Natural Language Processing*, pages 1535–1545, 2011. 83

Ronald Fagin, Laura M. Haas, Mauricio A. Hernández, Renée J. Miller, Lucian Popa, and Yannis Velegrakis. Clio: Schema mapping creation and data exchange. In Alexander T. Borgida, Vinay K. Chaudhri, Paolo Giorgini, and Eric S. Yu, editors, *Conceptual Modeling: Foundations and Applications*, pages 198–236. Springer, 2009. DOI: 10.1007/978-3-642-02463-4 40

Ronald Fagin, Phokion G. Kolaitis, Renée J. Miller, and Lucian Popa. Data exchange: Semantics and query answering. *Theor. Comp. Sci.*, 336(1):89–124, 2005a. DOI: 10.1016/j.tcs.2004.10.033 36, 39, 41, 42, 43, 52

Ronald Fagin, Phokion G. Kolaitis, and Lucian Popa. Data exchange: Getting to the core. *ACM Trans. Database Syst.*, 30(1):174–210, 2005b. DOI: 10.1145/1061318.1061323 43

R. Feldman and J. Sanger. *The Text Mining Handbook: Advanced Approaches in Analyzing Unstructured Data*. Cambridge University Press, 2007. 105

Stephen Few. *Information dashboard design: the effective visual communication of data*. O'Reilly, 2006. 94, 96, 97, 98, 99

Stephen Few. *Now You See It: Simple Visualization Techniques for Quantitative Analysis*. Analytics Press, 2009. 104

Richard Fikes. Ontologies: What are they, and where's the research? In *Proc. 5th Int. Conf. Principles of Knowledge Representation and Reasoning*, pages 652–653, 1996. 57

Jenny Rose Finkel, Trond Grenager, and Christopher Manning. Incorporating non-local information into information extraction systems by gibbs sampling. In *Proc. 43rd Annual Meeting Assoc. for Computational Linguistics*, pages 363–370, 2005. DOI: 10.3115/1219840.1219885 78

George H. L. Fletcher and Catharine M. Wyss. Towards a general framework for effective solutions to the data mapping problem. *J. Data Semantics*, 14:37–73, 2009. DOI: 10.1007/978-3-642-10562-3_2 44

Enrico Franconi, Nhung Ngo, and Evgeny Sherkhonov. The definability abduction problem for data exchange. In Markus Krötzsch and Umberto Straccia, editors, *Web Reasoning and Rule Systems*, pages 217–220. Springer, 2012. DOI: 10.1007/978-3-642-33203-6 43

Gottlob Frege. *The Foundations of Arithmetic*. Northwestern University Press, 1980. English translation by J.L. Austin. 49

C Friedman, P Kra, H Yu, M Krauthammer, and A Rzhetsky. GENIES: a natural-language processing system for the extraction of molecular pathways from journal articles. *Bioinformatics*, 17 Suppl 1:S74–82, 2001. DOI: 10.1093/bioinformatics/17.suppl_1.S74 90

Marc Friedman, Alon Levy, and Todd Millstein. Navigational plans for data integration. In *Proc. 16th National Conf. on Artificial Intelligence and 11th Innovative Applications of Artificial Intelligence Conf.*, pages 67–73, 1999. 58

Ariel Fuxman, Elham Fazli, and Renée J. Miller. ConQuer: efficient management of inconsistent databases. *Proc. ACM SIGMOD Int. Conf. on Management of Data*, pages 155–166, 2005. DOI: 10.1145/1066157.1066176 44

Ariel Fuxman, Mauricio A. Hernández, C. T. Howard Ho, Renée J. Miller, Paolo Papotti, and Lucian Popa. Nested mappings: Schema mapping reloaded. In *Proc. 32nd Int. Conf. on Very Large Data Bases*, pages 67–78, 2006. 43

Ariel Fuxman and Renée J. Miller. First-order query rewriting for inconsistent databases. *J. Comp. and System Sci.*, 73(4):610–635, 2007. DOI: 10.1016/j.jcss.2006.10.013 44

Helena Galhardas, Daniela Florescu, Dennis Shasha, Eric Simon, and Cristian-Augustin Saita. Declarative data cleaning: Language, model, and algorithms. In *Proc. 27th Int. Conf. on Very Large Data Bases*, pages 371–380, 2001. 45

César A. Galindo-Legaria. Outerjoins as disjunctions. In *Proc. ACM SIGMOD Int. Conf. on Management of Data*, pages 348–358, 1994. DOI: 10.1145/191843.191908 45

Philippe Gambette and Jean Veronis. Visualising a text with a tree cloud. In *Classification as a Tool for Research – Classification as a Tool for Research – Proc. 11th IFCS Biennial Conf. and 33rd Annual Conf of the Gesellschaft für Klassifikation*, pages 561–569, 2009. 105, 106

M. Gardner, J. Lutes, J. Lund an J. Hansen, D. Walker, E. Ringger, and K. Seppi. The topic browser an interactive tool for browsing topic models. In *Proc. NIPS Workshop on Challenges of Data Visualization*, 2010. 109

Paolo Giorgini, John Mylopoulos, Eleonora Nicchiarelli, and Roberto Sebastiani. Formal reasoning techniques for goal models. *J. on Data Semant.*, 1:1–20, 2004. DOI: 10.1007/978-3-540-39733-5_1 32

Jaap Gordijn and J. M. Akkermans. Value-based requirements engineering: exploring innovative e-commerce ideas. *Requir. Eng.*, 8(2):114–134, 2003. DOI: 10.1007/s00766-003-0169-x 27

Georg Gottlob, Reinhard Pichler, and Vadim Savenkov. Normalization and optimization of schema mappings. *VLDB J.*, 20(2):277–302, 2011. DOI: 10.1007/s00778-011-0226-x 43

Georg Gottlob and Pierre Senellart. Schema mapping discovery from data instances. *J. ACM*, 57 (2), 2010. DOI: 10.1145/1667053.1667055 44

Jim Gray, Adam Bosworth, Andrew Layman, and Hamid Pirahesh. Data cube: A relational aggregation operator generalizing group-by, cross-tab, and sub-total. In *Proc. 12th Int. Conf. on Data Engineering*, pages 152–159, 1996. DOI: 10.1109/ICDE.1996.492099 61

Sergio Greco, Luigi Pontieri, and Ester Zumpano. Integrating and managing conflicting data. In Dines Bjørner, Manfred Broy, and Alexandre Zamulin, editors, *Perspectives of System Informatics*, pages 349–362. Springer, 2001. DOI: 10.1007/3-540-45575-2 45

Michelle L. Gregory, Nancy Chinchor, Paul Whitney, Richard Carter, Elizabeth Hetzler, and Alan Turner. User-directed sentiment analysis: Visualizing the affective content of documents. In *Proc. Workshop on Sentiment and Subjectivity in Text*, pages 23–30, 2006. DOI: 10.3115/1654641.1654645 114, 115

Brynjar Gretarsson, John O'Donovan, Svetlin Bostandjiev, Tobias Höllerer, Arthur Asuncion, David Newman, and Padhraic Smyth. Topicnets: Visual analysis of large text corpora with topic modeling. *ACM Trans. Intell. Syst. Technol.*, 3(2):Article 23, 2012. DOI: 10.1145/2089094.2089099 109

Henning Griethe. Visualizing uncertainty for improved decision making. In *Proc. 4th Int. Conf. Perspectives in Business Informatics Research*, 2005. 103

Ralph Grishman and Beth Sundheim. Message understanding conference-6: a brief history. In *Proc. 16th Int. Conf. on Computational Linguistics*, pages 466–471, 1996. DOI: 10.3115/992628.992709 89

J. Gruser. Wrapper generation for web accessible data sources. In *Proc. Int. Conf. on Cooperative Inf. Syst.*, pages 14–23, 1998. 59

Alon Y. Halevy, Naveen Ashish, Dina Bitton, Michael Carey, Denise Draper, Jeff Pollock, Arnon Rosenthal, and Vishal Sikka. Enterprise information integration: successes, challenges and controversies. In *Proc. ACM SIGMOD Int. Conf. on Management of Data*, pages 778–787, 2005. DOI: 10.1145/1066157.1066246 65

Alon Y. Halevy, Zachary G. Ives, Dan Suciu, and Igor Tatarinov. Piazza: Data management infrastructure for semantic web applications. In *Proc. 19th Int. Conf. on Data Engineering*, pages 505–516, 2003. DOI: 10.1145/775152.775231 64

Michael Hammer. Reengineering work: Don't automate, obliterate. *Harvard Bus. Rev.*, 68:104–112, 1990. 22

Joachim Hammer, Hector Garcia-Molina, Svetlozar Nestorov, Ramana Yerneni, Markus M. Breunig, and Vasilis Vassalos. Template-based wrappers in the tsimmis system (system demonstration). In *Proc. ACM SIGMOD Int. Conf. on Management of Data*, 1997. DOI: 10.1145/253262.253395 59

M. Hammond. The fact gap: the disconnect between data and decisions – a study of executives in the United States and Europe. Technical report, Business Objects, 2004. (Last checked December 2012). 7

Takaaki Hasegawa, Satoshi Sekine, and Ralph Grishman. Discovering relations among named entities from large corpora. In *Proc. 42nd Annual Meeting Assoc. for Computational Linguistics*, 2004. DOI: 10.3115/1218955.1219008 83

S. Havre, B. Hetzler, and L. Nowell. Themeriver: visualizing theme changes over time. In *Proc. IEEE Symp. Information Visualization*, pages 115–123, 2000. DOI: 10.1109/INFVIS.2000.885098 109, 110

Robert V. Head. Getting Sabre off the ground. *IEEE Annals of the History of Comp.*, 24(4):32–39, 2002. DOI: 10.1109/MAHC.2002.1114868 54

Marti A. Hearst. Automatic acquisition of hyponyms from large text corpora. In *Proc. 14th Int. Conf. on Computational Linguistics*, volume 2, pages 539–545, 1992. DOI: 10.3115/992133.992154 71, 72

Jeffrey Heer, Fernanda B. Viégas, and Martin Wattenberg. Voyagers and voyeurs: Supporting asynchronous collaborative visualization. *Commun. ACM*, 52(1):87–97, 2009. DOI: 10.1145/1435417.1435439 104

Mauricio A. Hernández and Salvatore J. Stolfo. Real-world Data is Dirty: Data Cleansing and The Merge/Purge Problem. *Data Mining and Knowledge Discovery*, 2(1):9–37, 1998. DOI: 10.1023/A:1009761603038 45

Johannes Hoffart, Fabian M. Suchanek, Klaus Berberich, and Gerhard Weikum. YAGO2: a spatially and temporally enhanced knowledge base from Wikipedia. *Artificial Intel.*, 194:28–61, 2013. DOI: 10.1016/j.artint.2012.06.001 90

Clemens Holzhüter, Alexander Lex, Dieter Schmalstieg, Hans-Jörg Schulz, Heidrun Schumann, and Marc Streit. Visualizing uncertainty in biological expression data. In *Proc. Visualization and Data Analysis 2012*, 2012. DOI: 10.1117/12.908516 103

Jennifer Horkoff, Alex Borgida, John Mylopoulos, Daniele Barone, Lei Jiang, Eric Yu, and Daniel Amyot. Making data meaningful: The business intelligence model and its formal semantics in description logics. In *On the Move to Meaningful Internet Systems–Proc. OTM Confederated Int. Conf. CoopIS, DOA, GADA, and ODBASE*, 2012. DOI: 10.1007/978-3-642-33615-7_17 32

Richard Hull and Masatoshi Yoshikawa. ILOG: declarative creation and manipulation of object identifiers. In *Proc. 16th Int. Conf. on Very Large Data Bases*, pages 455–468, 1990. 40

Tomasz Imielinski and Witold Lipski. Incomplete information and dependencies in relational databases. In *Proc. ACM SIGMOD Int. Conf. on Management of Data*, pages 178–184, 1983. DOI: 10.1145/971695.582222 37, 43

William H. Inmon and Anthony Nesavich. *Tapping into Unstructured Data: Integrating Unstructured Data and Textual Analytics into Business Intelligence*. Prentice Hall, 2007. 89

Panagiotis G. Ipeirotis, Eugene Agichtein, Pranay Jain, and Luis Gravano. To search or to crawl?: towards a query optimizer for text-centric tasks. In *Proc. ACM SIGMOD Int. Conf. on Management of Data*, pages 265–276, 2006. DOI: 10.1145/1142473.1142504 88

Zachary Ives, Daniela Florescu, Marc Friedman, Alon Levy, and Dan Weld. An adaptive query execution engine for data integration. In *Proc. ACM SIGMOD Int. Conf. on Management of Data*, 1999. DOI: 10.1145/304181.304209 58

Alpa Jain, AnHai Doan, and Luis Gravano. Optimizing SQL queries over text databases. In *Proc. 24th Int. Conf. on Data Engineering*, pages 636–645, 2008. DOI: 10.1109/ICDE.2008.4497472 88

Lei Jiang, Daniele Barone, Daniel Amyot, and John Mylopoulos. Strategic models for business intelligence: Reasoning about opportunities and threats. In *Proc. 30th Int. Conf. on Conceptual Modeling*, pages 429–443, 2011a. 32

Lei Jiang, Daniele Barone, Daniel Amyot, and John Mylopoulos. Strategic models for business intelligence. In *Proc. 30th Int. Conf. on Conceptual Modeling*, pages 429–439, 2011b. DOI: 10.1007/978-3-642-24606-7_33 33, 40

Daniel Jurafsky. *Speech and Language Processing*. Prentice Hall, 2nd edition, 2008. 67

Robert S. Kaplan and David P. Norton. The balanced scorecard – measures that drive performance the balanced scorecard – measures. *Harvard Bus. Rev.*, 70(1):71–79, 1992. 22, 28

Robert S. Kaplan and David P. Norton. Having trouble with your strategy? Map it. *Harvard Bus. Rev.*, (September-October):1–12, 2000. 23, 28

KyungTae Kim, Sungahn Ko, Niklas Elmqvist, and David S. Ebert. Wordbridge: Using composite tag clouds in node-link diagrams for visualizing content and relations in text corpora. In *Proc. 44th Annual Hawaii Int. Conf. on System Sciences*, pages 1–8, 2011. DOI: 10.1109/HICSS.2011.499 107, 108

Jon Kleinberg. Bursty and hierarchical structure in streams. In *Proc. 8th ACM SIGKDD Int. Conf. on Knowledge Discovery and Data Mining*, pages 91–101, 2002. DOI: 10.1145/775047.775061 110

Zornitsa Kozareva and Eduard H. Hovy. A semi-supervised method to learn and construct taxonomies using the web. In *Proc. 2010 Conf. on Empirical Methods in Natural Language Processing*, pages 1110–1118, 2010. 79

William L. Kuechler. Business applications of unstructured text. *Commun. ACM*, 50(10):86–93, 2007. DOI: 10.1145/1290958.1290967 67

N. Kushmerick, R. Doorenbos, and D. Weld. Wrapper induction for information extraction. In *Proc. 15th Int. Joint Conf. on AI*, volume 1, pages 729–737, 1997. 59

John D. Lafferty, Andrew McCallum, and Fernando C. N. Pereira. Conditional random fields: Probabilistic models for segmenting and labeling sequence data. In *Proc. 18th Int. Conf. on Machine Learning*, pages 282–289, 2001. 73

Maurizio Lenzerini. Data integration: A theoretical perspective. In *Proc. 21st ACM SIGACT-SIGMOD-SIGART Symp. on Principles of Database Systems*, pages 233–246, 2002. DOI: 10.1145/543613.543644 58

E Letier and Axel Van Lamsweerde. Reasoning about partial goal satisfaction for requirements and design engineering. *ACM SIGSOFT Softw. Eng. Notes*, 29(6):53–62, 2004. DOI: 10.1145/1041685.1029905 32

Hector J. Levesque. Making believers out of computers. *Artificial Intel.*, 30(1):81–108, 1986. DOI: 10.1016/0004-3702(86)90068-8 34, 37, 38, 52

Alon Y. Levy, Alberto O. Mendelzon, Yehoshua Sagiv, and Divesh Srivastava. Answering queries using views. In *Proc. 14th ACM SIGACT-SIGMOD-SIGART Symp. on Principles of Database Systems*, pages 95–104, 1995. DOI: 10.1007/s007780100054 60

Alon Y. Levy, Anand Rajaraman, and Joann J. Ordille. Query answering algorithms for information agents. In *Proc. 13th National Conf. on Artificial Intelligence and 8th Innovative Applications of Artificial Intelligence Conf.*, 1996a. 61

Alon Y. Levy, Anand Rajaraman, and Joann J. Ordille. Querying heterogeneous information sources using source descriptions. In *Proc. 22th Int. Conf. on Very Large Data Bases*, pages 251–262, 1996b. 57, 58, 59

Leonid Libkin. Data exchange and incomplete information. In *Proc. 25th ACM SIGACT-SIGMOD-SIGART Symp. on Principles of Database Systems*, pages 60–69, 2006. DOI: 10.1145/1142351.1142360 46

Cindy Xide Lin, Bolin Ding, Jiawei Han, Feida Zhu, and Bo Zhao. Text Cube: Computing IR measures for multidimensional text database analysis. In *Proc. 2008 IEEE Int. Conf. on Data Mining*, pages 905–910, 2008. DOI: 10.1109/ICDM.2008.135 69

David S. Linthicum. *Enterprise Application Integration*. Addison-Wesley Professional, 2000. 66

Bing Liu. *Sentiment Analysis and Opinion Mining*. Synthesis Lectures on Human Language Technologies. Morgan & Claypool Publishers, 2012. DOI: 10.2200/S00416ED1V01Y201204HLT016 105, 114

Ling Liu, Calton Pu, and Wei Han. XWRAP: An XML-enabled wrapper construction system for web information sources. In *Proc. 16th Int. Conf. on Data Engineering*, pages 611–621, 2000. DOI: 10.1109/ICDE.2000.839475 85

Shixia Liu, Michelle X. Zhou, Shimei Pan, Yangqiu Song, Weihong Qian, Weijia Cai, and Xiaoxiao Lian. Tiara: Interactive, topic-based visual text summarization and analysis. *ACM Trans. Intell. Syst. Technol.*, 3(2):Article 25, 2012. DOI: 10.1145/2089094.2089101 110

S. Lohmann, J. Ziegler, and L. Tetzlaff. Comparison of tag cloud layouts: Task-related performance and visual exploration. In *Proc. 12th IFIP TC 13 Int. Conf. on Human-Computer Interaction: Part I*, pages 392–404, 2009. DOI: 10.1007/978-3-642-03655-2_43 105

H. P. Luhn. A business intelligence systems. *IBM Systems J.*, 2(3):314–319, 1958. DOI: 10.1147/rd.24.0314 1

C. Manning, P. Raghavan, and H. Schuetze. *Introduction to Information Retrieval*. Cambridge University Press, 2008. DOI: 10.1017/CBO9780511809071 105

Imran R. Mansuri and Sunita Sarawagi. Integrating unstructured data into relational databases. In *Proc. 22nd Int. Conf. on Data Engineering*, page 29, 2006. DOI: 10.1109/ICDE.2006.83 82, 87, 88

Bruno Marnette, Giansalvatore Mecca, and Paolo Papotti. Scalable data exchange with functional dependencies. *Proc. VLDB Endowment*, 3(1):105–116, 2010. 43

Bruno Marnette, Giansalvatore Mecca, Paolo Papotti, Salvatore Raunich, and Donatello Santoro. ++Spicy: an OpenSource tool for second-generation schema mapping and data exchange. *Proc. VLDB Endowment*, 4(12):1438–1441, 2011. 40

Andrew McCallum. Information extraction: Distilling structured data from unstructured text. *Queue*, 3(9):48–57, 2005. DOI: 10.1145/1105664.1105679 82

William E. McCarthy. The REA accounting model: A generalized framework for accounting systems in a shared data environment. *Accounting Rev.*, 57(3):554–554, 1982. 27

Giansalvatore Mecca, Paolo Papotti, and Salvatore Raunich. Core schema mappings. In *Proc. ACM SIGMOD Int. Conf. on Management of Data*, pages 655–668, 2009. DOI: 10.1145/1559845.1559914 43

Yuval Merhav, Filipe Mesquita, Denilson Barbosa, Wai Gen Yee, and Ophir Frieder. Extracting Information Networks from the Blogosphere. *ACM Trans. Web*, 6(3):11:1–11:33, 2012. DOI: 10.1145/2344416.2344418 83, 84

Matthew Michelson and Craig A. Knoblock. Creating relational data from unstructured and ungrammatical data sources. *J. Artificial Intel. Res.*, 31(1):543–590, 2008. DOI: 10.1613/jair.2409 89

George A. Miller. WordNet: a lexical database for English. *Commun. ACM*, 38(11):39–41, 1995. DOI: 10.1145/219717.219748 79

David Milne and Ian H. Witten. Learning to link with wikipedia. In *Proc. 17th ACM Int. Conf. on Information and Knowledge Management*, pages 509–518, 2008. DOI: 10.1145/1458082.1458150 76

G. Moore. Enterprises shifting from 'systems of record' to 'systems of engagement'. In *The Future of Enterprise IT Innovation Conference*, 2011. 15

John Mylopoulos. Information modeling in the time of the revolution. *Inf. Syst.*, 23(3-4):127–155, 1998. DOI: 10.1016/S0306-4379(98)00005-2 19

David Nadeau and Satoshi Sekine. A survey of named entity recognition and classification. *Lingvisticae Investigationes*, 30(1):3–26, 2007. DOI: 10.1075/li.30.1.03nad 74, 89

Felix Naumann. *Quality-Driven Query Answering for Integrated Information Systems*, volume 2261 of *Lecture Notes in Computer Science*. Springer, 2002. DOI: 10.1007/3-540-45921-9 45

Object Management Group. Business motivation model, version 1.0. Technical report, Object Management Group, May 2002. 28

Chris Olston and Jock D. Mackinlay. Visualizing data with bounded uncertainty. In *Proc. IEEE Symp. Information Visualization*, pages 37–40, 2002. DOI: 10.1109/INFVIS.2002.1173145 103

Alexander Osterwalder. *The Business Model Ontology - a proposition in a design science approach*. PhD thesis, HEC Lausanne, 2004. 25

A. Osterwalder and Y. Pigneur. *Business Model Generation*. Self Published, 2009. Available at http://www.businessmodelgeneration.com/book. 24

Bo Pang and Lillian Lee. Opinion mining and sentiment analysis. *Foundations and Trends in Information Retrieval*, 2(1-2):1–135, 2008. DOI: 10.1561/1500000011 113

Alex T. Pang, Craig M. Wittenbrink, and Suresh K. Lodha. Approaches to uncertainty visualization. *The Visual Computer*, 13:370–390, 1997. DOI: 10.1007/s003710050111 103

Yannis Papakonstantinou, Serge Abiteboul, and Hector Garcia-Molina. Object fusion in mediator systems. In *Proc. 22th Int. Conf. on Very Large Data Bases*, pages 413–424, 1996. 40

David Parmenter. *Key Performance Indicators*. John Wiley & Sons, 2007. 30

Marius Paşca, Dekang Lin, Jeffrey Bigham, Andrei Lifchits, and Alpa Jain. Organizing and searching the world wide web of facts - step one: the one-million fact extraction challenge. In *Proc. 21st National Conf. on Artificial Intelligence and 18th Innovative Applications of Artificial Intelligence Conf.*, pages 1400–1405, 2006. 82

Marco Pennacchiotti and Patrick Pantel. Entity extraction via ensemble semantics. In *Proc. 2009 Conf. on Empirical Methods in Natural Language Processing*, volume 1, pages 238–247, 2009. 77

Juan Manuel Pérez-Martínez, Rafael Berlanga-Llavori, María José Aramburu-Cabo, and Torben Bach Pedersen. Contextualizing data warehouses with documents. *Decis. Support Syst.*, 45(1):77–94, 2008. DOI: 10.1016/j.dss.2006.12.005 69

William Pike, Joe Bruce, Bob Baddeley, Daniel Best, Lyndsey Franklin, Richard May, Douglas Rice, Rick Riensche, and Katarina Younkin. The scalable reasoning system: lightweight visualization for distributed analytics. *Information Visualization*, 8(1):71–84, 2009. DOI: 10.1057/ivs.2008.33 119

H. Plattner. A common database approach for oltp and olap using an in-memory column database. In *Proc. ACM SIGMOD Int. Conf. on Management of Data*, pages 1–2, 2009. DOI: 10.1145/1559845.1559846 14

H. Plattner and A. Zeier. *In-Memory Data Management: An Inflection Point for Enterprise Applications*. Springer, 2011. 15

Lucian Popa, Yannis Velegrakis, Renée J. Miller, Mauricio A. Hernández, and Ronald Fagin. Translating web data. In *Proc. 28th Int. Conf. on Very Large Data Bases*, pages 598–609, 2002. DOI: 10.1016/B978-155860869-6/50059-7 39, 40, 52

M. Porter. *Competitive Strategy: Techniques for Analyzing Industries and Competitors*. The Free Press, New York, USA, 1980. 24

Rachel A. Pottinger and Alon Y. Halevy. Minicon: A scalable algorithm for answering queries using views. *VLDB J.*, 10(2-3):182–198, 2001. DOI: 10.1007/s007780100048 58, 60

Trivellore E. Raghunathan. What do we do with missing data? some options for analysis of incomplete data. *Annu. Rev. Public Health*, 25:99–117, 2004. DOI: 10.1146/annurev.publhealth.25.102802.124410 44

Karthik Raghunathan, Heeyoung Lee, Sudarshan Rangarajan, Nathanael Chambers, Mihai Surdeanu, Dan Jurafsky, and Christopher Manning. A multi-pass sieve for coreference resolution. In *Proc. 2010 Conf. on Empirical Methods in Natural Language Processing*, pages 492–501, 2010. 76

L. Ratinov and D. Roth. Design challenges and misconceptions in named entity recognition. In *Proc. 13th Conf. on Computational Natural Language Learning*, 2009. 75

Lev Ratinov, Dan Roth, Doug Downey, and Mike Anderson. Local and global algorithms for disambiguation to Wikipedia. In *Proc. 49th Annual Meeting Assoc. for Computational Linguistics*, volume 1, pages 1375–1384, 2011. 76

Sujith Ravi and Marius Paşca. Using structured text for large-scale attribute extraction. In *Proc. 17th ACM Int. Conf. on Information and Knowledge Management*, pages 1183–1192, 2008. DOI: 10.1145/1458082.1458238 82, 87

Darrell R. Raymond, Frank Wm. Tompa, and Derick Wood. From data representation to data model: Meta-semantic issues in the evolution of sgml. *Computer Standards & Interfaces*, 18(1): 25–36, 1996. DOI: 10.1016/0920-5489(96)00033-5 68

Lívia de S. Ribeiro, Ronaldo R. Goldschmidt, and Maria Cláudia Cavalcanti. Complementing data in the ETL process. In *Proc. 13th Int. Conf. Data Warehousing and Knowledge Discovery*, pages 112–123, 2011. DOI: 10.1007/978-3-642-23544-3_9 44

Christian Rohrdantz, Annette Hautli, Thomas Mayer, Miriam Butt, Daniel A. Keim, and Frans Plank. Towards tracking semantic change by visual analytics. In *Proc. 49th Annual Meeting Assoc. for Computational Linguistics*, pages 305–310, 2011. 112, 113

Ronald G. Ross. Modeling business rules. In Sanjiv Purba, editor, *High-Performance Web Databases*, pages 145–155. CRC Press, 2001. ISBN 0-8493-0882-8. 51

P. Russom. TDWI best practices report: Big data analytics. Technical report, The data Warehousing Institute, 2011. 13

Horacio Saggion, Adam Funk, Diana Maynard, and Kalina Bontcheva. Ontology-based information extraction for business intelligence. In *Proc. 6th Int. Semantic Web Conf. and 2nd Asian Conf. on Asian Semantic Web Conf.*, pages 843–856, 2007. DOI: 10.1007/978-3-540-76298-0_61 69

Erik F. Tjong Kim Sang and Fien De Meulder. Introduction to the CoNLL-2003 shared task: language-independent named entity recognition. In *Proc. Conf. on Human Language Technology Conference of the North American Chapter of the Association of Computational Linguistics*, pages 142–147, 2003. DOI: 10.3115/1119176.1119195 74

Sunita Sarawagi. Information extraction. *Foundations and Trends in Databases*, 1(3):261–377, 2008. 89

Sunita Sarawagi and William W. Cohen. Semi-Markov conditional random fields for information extraction. In *Advances in Neural Information Proc. Systems 17, Proc. Neural Information Proc. Systems*, pages 1185–1192, 2004. 87

Kunal Sengupta, Adila Alfa Krisnadhi, and Pascal Hitzler. Local closed world semantics: Grounded circumscription for OWL. In *Proc. 10th Int. Semantic Web Conf.*, pages 617–632, 2011. DOI: 10.1007/978-3-642-25073-6_39 46

Ben Shneiderman. The eyes have it: A task by data type taxonomy for information visualizations. In *Proc. IEEE Symp. Visual Languages*, pages 336–343, 1996. DOI: 10.1109/VL.1996.545307 93

Yannis Sismanis, Ling Wang, Ariel Fuxman, Peter J. Haas, and Berthold Reinwald. Resolution-aware query answering for business intelligence. In *Proc. 25th Int. Conf. on Data Engineering*, pages 976–987, 2009. DOI: 10.1109/ICDE.2009.81 45, 50

Rion Snow, Daniel Jurafsky, and Andrew Y. Ng. Learning Syntactic Patterns for Automatic Hypernym Discovery. In *Advances in Neural Information Proc. Systems 17, Proc. Neural Information Proc. Systems*, pages 1297–1304. MIT Press, 2005. 73, 79, 80

Stephen Soderland. Learning information extraction rules for semi-structured and free text. *Machine Learning*, 34(1-3):233–272, 1999. DOI: 10.1023/A:1007562322031 89

John Stasko, Carsten Gorg, Zhicheng Liu, and Kanupriya Singhal. Jigsaw: Supporting investigative analysis through interactive visualization. In *Proc. IEEE Symp. on Visual Analytics Science and Technology*, pages 131–138, 2007. DOI: 10.1109/VAST.2007.4389006 120

Slawek Staworko, Jan Chomicki, and Jerzy Marcinkowski. Prioritized repairing and consistent query answering in relational databases. *Ann. Math. Artif. Intell.*, 64(2-3):209–246, 2012. DOI: 10.1007/s10472-012-9288-8 44

Mark Steyvers, Padhraic Smyth, Michal Rosen-Zvi, and Thomas Griffiths. Probabilistic author-topic models for information discovery. In *Proc. 10th ACM SIGKDD Int. Conf. on Knowledge Discovery and Data Mining*, pages 306–315, 2004. DOI: 10.1145/1014052.1014087 108

Florian Stroh, Robert Winter, and Felix Wortmann. Method support of information requirements analysis for analytical information systems. *Bus. Inf. Syst. Eng.*, 3(1):33–43, 2011. DOI: 10.1007/s12599-010-0138-0 28

Fabian M. Suchanek, Georgiana Ifrim, and Gerhard Weikum. Combining linguistic and statistical analysis to extract relations from web documents. In *Proc. 12th ACM SIGKDD Int. Conf. on Knowledge Discovery and Data Mining*, pages 712–717, 2006. DOI: 10.1145/1150402.1150492 84

Balder ten Cate, Laura Chiticariu, Phokion G. Kolaitis, and Wang Chiew Tan. Laconic schema mappings: Computing the core with SQL queries. *Proc. VLDB Endowment*, 2(1):1006–1017, 2009. 43

Pradeep B. Teregowda, Madian Khabsa, and Clyde L. Giles. A system for indexing tables, algorithms and figures. In *Proc. 12th ACM/IEEE Joint Conf. on Digital Libraries*, pages 343–344, 2012. DOI: 10.1145/2232817.2232882 90

M. Treacy and F. Wiersema. *The Discipline of Market Leaders: Choose your customers, narrow your focus, dominate your market*. Addison-Wesley, Reading, USA, 1997. 24

Frank S. C. Tseng and Annie Y. H. Chou. The concept of document warehousing for multi-dimensional modeling of textual-based business intelligence. *Decis. Support Syst.*, 42(2):727–744, 2006. DOI: 10.1016/j.dss.2005.02.011 69

Mikalai Tsytsarau and Themis Palpanas. Survey on mining subjective data on the web. *Data Mining and Knowledge Discovery*, 24(3):478–514, 2012. DOI: 10.1007/s10618-011-0238-6 113

Wil M. P. van der Aalst. Formalization and verification of event-driven process chains. *Inf. and Softw. Tech.*, 41(10):639–650, 1999. DOI: 10.1016/S0950-5849(99)00016-6 22

Wil M. P. van der Aalst. *Process Mining: Discovery, Conformance and Enhancement of Business Processes.* Springer, 2011. 46, 51

Frank van Ham, Martin Wattenberg, and Fernanda B. Viégas. Mapping text with phrase nets. *IEEE Trans. Visualization and Comp. Graphics*, 15(6):1169–1176, 2009. DOI: 10.1109/TVCG.2009.165 123

Yannis Velegrakis, Renée J. Miller, and Lucian Popa. Mapping adaptation under evolving schemas. In *Proc. 29th Int. Conf. on Very Large Data Bases*, pages 584–595, 2003. 44

D. Vesset, B. McDonough, and M. Wardley. Worldwide business analytics software 2010-2014 forecast and 2009 vendor shares. Technical report, IDC, 2010. 7

Fernanda B. Viégas, Scott Golder, and Judith Donath. Visualizing email content: portraying relationships from conversational histories. In *Proc. SIGCHI Conf. on Human Factors in Computing Systems*, pages 979–988, 2006. DOI: 10.1145/1124772.1124919 112

Fernanda B. Viégas, Martin Wattenberg, and Jonathan Feinberg. Participatory visualization with wordle. *IEEE Trans. Visualization and Comp. Graphics*, 15(6):1137–1144, 2009. DOI: 10.1109/TVCG.2009.171 105, 107

Fernanda B. Viégas, Martin Wattenberg, Frank van Ham, Jesse Kriss, and Matt McKeon. Manyeyes: a site for visualization at internet scale. *IEEE Trans. Visualization and Comp. Graphics*, 13(6):1121–1128, 2007. DOI: 10.1109/TVCG.2007.70577 104

Richard C. Wang and William W. Cohen. Iterative Set Expansion of Named Entities Using the Web. In *Proc. 2008 IEEE Int. Conf. on Data Mining*, pages 1091–1096, 2008. DOI: 10.1109/ICDM.2008.145 77

P. Weill, T. Malone, V. D'Urso, G. Herman, and S. Woerner. Do some business models perform better than others? a study of the 1000 largest US firms. Technical Report Working paper n.226, Sloan School of Management, MIT, 2005. 25

Stephen A. White and Derek Miers. *BPMN Modeling and Reference Guide.* Future Strategies Inc., 2008. 20

Michael Wick, Aron Culotta, and Andrew McCallum. Learning field compatibilities to extract database records from unstructured text. In *Proc. 2006 Conf. on Empirical Methods in Natural Language Processing*, pages 603–611, 2006. DOI: 10.3115/1610075.1610160 84

Fei Wu, Raphael Hoffmann, and Daniel S. Weld. Information extraction from Wikipedia: moving down the long tail. In *Proc. 14th ACM SIGKDD Int. Conf. on Knowledge Discovery and Data Mining*, pages 731–739, 2008. DOI: 10.1145/1401890.1401978 82, 84, 91

Ling-Ling Yan, Renée J. Miller, Laura M. Haas, and Ronald Fagin. Data-driven understanding and refinement of schema mappings. In *Proc. ACM SIGMOD Int. Conf. on Management of Data*, pages 485–496, 2001. DOI: 10.1145/376284.375729 44

Ling-Ling Yan and M. Tamer Özsu. Conflict tolerant queries in AURORA. In *Proc. Int. Conf. on Cooperative Inf. Syst.*, pages 279–290, 1999. DOI: 10.1109/COOPIS.1999.792177 45

Koji Yatani, Michael Novati, Andrew Trusty, and Khai N. Truong. Review spotlight: a user interface for summarizing user-generated reviews using adjective-noun word pairs. In *Proc. SIGCHI Conf. on Human Factors in Computing Systems*, pages 1541–1550, 2011. DOI: 10.1145/1978942.1979167 114, 116

Alexander Yates and Oren Etzioni. Unsupervised resolution of objects and relations on the web. In *Proc. Conf. on Human Language Technology Conference of the North American Chapter of the Association of Computational Linguistics*, pages 121–130, 2007. 84

Xiaoxin Yin, Wenzhao Tan, and Chao Liu. FACTO: a fact lookup engine based on web tables. In *Proc. 20th Int. World Wide Web Conf.*, pages 507–516, 2011. DOI: 10.1145/1963405.1963477 86

Cong Yu and Lucian Popa. Semantic adaptation of schema mappings when schemas evolve. In *Proc. 31st Int. Conf. on Very Large Data Bases*, pages 1006–1017, 2005. 44

Eric Yu. Towards modelling and reasoning support for early-phase requirements engineering. In *Proc. 3rd IEEE Int. Symp. on Requirements Engineering*, volume 97, pages 226–235, 1997. DOI: 10.1109/ISRE.1997.566873 30

Yanhong Zhai and Bing Liu. Web data extraction based on partial tree alignment. In *Proc. 14th Int. World Wide Web Conf.*, pages 76–85, 2005. DOI: 10.1145/1060745.1060761 86

Qi Zhang, Fabian M. Suchanek, Lihua Yue, and Gerhard Weikum. TOB: timely ontologies for business relations. In *Proc. 11th Int. Workshop on the World Wide Web and Databases*, 2008. 84

Authors' Biographies

RAYMOND T. NG

Dr. Raymond T. Ng is a Professor of Computer Science at the University of British Columbia. He received a Ph.D. in Computer Science from the University of Maryland in 1992. His main research area for the past two decades is on data mining, with a specific focus on health informatics and text mining. He has published over 150 peer-reviewed publications on data clustering, outlier detection, OLAP processing, health informatics, and text mining. He is the recipient of two best paper awards, from the 2001 ACM SIGKDD conference, which is the premier data mining conference worldwide, and the 2005 ACM SIGMOD conference, which is one of the top database conferences worldwide. He was a program co-chair of the 2009 International Conference on Data Engineering, and a program co-chair of the 2002 ACM SIGKDD conference. He was also one of the general co-chairs of the 2008 ACM SIGMOD conference. He was an editorial board member of the Very Large Database Journal and the IEEE Transactions on Knowledge and Data Engineering until 2008.

PATRICIA C. AROCENA

Patricia C. Arocena is a Research Assistant in Computer Science at the University of Toronto. She received her M.Eng. in Electrical and Computer Engineering in 2001 and her Ph.D. in Computer Science (expected 2013), both from the University of Toronto. Her research focuses on developing techniques to support efficient and practical use of schema mappings in information integration, and in particular, on embracing *incompleteness* in the context of data-driven decision making.

DENILSON BARBOSA

Denilson Barbosa is an Associate Professor of Computing Science at the University of Alberta. He obtained a Ph.D. in 2005 from the University of Toronto, working on Web data management. He received an IBM Faculty Award for his work on XML benchmarking, and an Alberta Ingenuity New Faculty Award for his work on extraction and integration of data from the Web. He received the Best Paper award at the 26th IEEE International Conference on Data Engineering (ICDE 2010). At the time of writing, he was a lead investigator on the NSERC Strategic Network on Business Intelligence, through which the SONEX system for large-scale relation extraction on the web is developed.

GIUSEPPE CARENINI

Giuseppe Carenini is an Associate Professor of Computer Science at the University of British Columbia. He is also an Associate member of the UBC Institute for Resources, Environment and Sustainability (IRES). Giuseppe has broad interdisciplinary interests. His work on natural language processing and information visualization to support decision making has been published in over 80 peer-reviewed papers. Dr. Carenini was the area chair for "Sentiment Analysis, Opinion Mining, and Text Classification" of ACL 2009 and the area chair for "Summarization and Generation" of NAACL 2012. He has recently co-edited an ACM-TIST Special Issue on "Intelligent Visual Interfaces for Text Analysis."
In July 2011, he published a co-authored book on *Methods for Mining and Summarizing Text Conversations*. In his work, Dr. Carenini has also extensively collaborated with industrial partners, including Microsoft and IBM. Giuseppe was awarded a Google Research Award and an IBM CASCON Best Exhibit Award in 2007 and 2010 respectively.

LUIZ GOMES, JR.

Luiz Gomes, Jr., is currently a Ph.D. student at the University of Campinas. Prior to that he conducted graduate research at the University of Waterloo and spent several years gaining research-oriented experience in industry and academia. He has worked in such diverse and exciting areas as information extraction, data mining, data integration, and complex network analysis.

STEPHAN JOU

Stephan Jou is currently a Technical Architect, Research Staff Member, and Sr. Manager at IBM's Business Analytics Office of the CTO, and has over fifteen years of experience designing, building, and inventing software from inception to release, from a small start-up to one of the largest software development companies in the world. In his career at Cognos and IBM, he has architected and led the development and productization of over ten 1.0 Cognos and IBM products in the areas of cloud computing, mobile, visualization, semantic search, data mining, and neural networks. His current role at IBM focuses on translating academic and IBM research into product strategy for the Business Analytics division at IBM. Stephan holds a M.Sc. in Computational Neuroscience and Biomedical Engineering, and a dual B.Sc. in Computer Science and Human Physiology, all from the University of Toronto.

ROCK ANTHONY LEUNG

Rock Anthony Leung is a Senior Researcher at SAP and manages its Academic Research Center (ARC), which initiates and supports collaborative research projects with academia. Through ARC, Rock actively works with graduate students, professors, and SAP stakeholders to explore and validate novel solutions in business intelligence, visual analytics, and other research areas. Rock is also a Scientific Advisory Committee member of the NSERC Business Intelligence Network. Rock earned a Ph.D. in Computer Science from the University of British Columbia (UBC), specializing in Human-Computer Interaction research. His research work has been published in numerous prominent journals and conferences. He has also actively contributed to several professional development programs at UBC and has received awards for his service and leadership.

EVANGELOS MILIOS

Evangelos Milios received a diploma in Electrical Engineering from the NTUA, Athens, Greece, and Master's and Ph.D. degrees in Electrical Engineering and Computer Science from the Massachusetts Institute of Technology. Since July of 1998 he has been with the Faculty of Computer Science, Dalhousie University, Halifax, Nova Scotia, where he served as Director of the Graduate Program (1999-2002) and as Associate Dean–Research since 2008. He is a Senior Member of the IEEE. He was a member of the ACM Dissertation Award committee (1990-1992), a member of the AAAI/SIGART Doctoral Consortium Committee (1997-2001), and he is co-editor-in-chief of Computational Intelligence. At Dalhousie, he held a Killam Chair of Computer Science (2006-2011). He has published on the interpretation of visual and range signals for landmark-based navigation and map construction in robotics. He currently works on modeling and mining of content and link structure of Networked Information Spaces, text mining, and visual text analytics.

RENÉE J. MILLER

Renée J. Miller is Professor and the Bell Canada Chair of Information Systems at the University of Toronto. She received BS degrees in Mathematics and in Cognitive Science from the Massachusetts Institute of Technology. She received her MS and Ph.D. degrees in Computer Science from the University of Wisconsin in Madison. She received the US Presidential Early Career Award for Scientists and Engineers (PECASE), the highest honor bestowed by the United States government on outstanding scientists and engineers beginning their careers. She received the National Science Foundation Early Career Award, is a Fellow of the ACM, the President of the VLDB Endowment, and was the Program Chair for ACM SIGMOD 2011 in Athens, Greece. She and her IBM co-authors received the ICDT Test-of-Time Award for their influential 2003 paper establishing the foundations of data exchange. Her research interests are in the efficient, effective use of large volumes of complex, heterogeneous data. This interest spans data integration, data exchange, knowledge curation and data sharing. In 2011, she was elected to the Fellowship of the Royal Society of Canada (FRSC), Canada's national academy.

JOHN MYLOPOULOS

John Mylopoulos holds a distinguished professor position (chiara fama) at the University of Trento, and a professor emeritus position at the University of Toronto. He earned a Ph.D. degree from Princeton University in 1970 and joined the Department of Computer Science at the University of Toronto that year. His research interests include conceptual modeling, requirements engineering, data semantics, and knowledge management. Mylopoulos is a fellow of the Association for the Advancement of Artificial Intelligence (AAAI) and the Royal Society of Canada (Academy of Sciences). He has served as program/general chair of international conferences in Artificial Intelligence, Databases and Software Engineering, including IJCAI (1991), Requirements Engineering (1997), and VLDB (2004).

RACHEL A. POTTINGER

Rachel A. Pottinger is an associate professor in Computer Science at the University of British Columbia. She received her Ph.D. in computer science from the University of Washington in 2004. Her main research interest is data management, particularly semantic data integration, how to manage metadata (i.e., data about data), and how to manage data that is currently not well supported by databases.

FRANK TOMPA

Frank Tompa has been a faculty member in computer science at the University of Waterloo since 1974. His teaching and research interests are in the fields of data structures and databases, particularly the design of text management systems suitable for maintaining large reference texts and large, heterogeneous text collections. He has co-authored papers in the areas of database dependency theory, storage structure selection, query processing, materialized view maintenance, text matching, XML processing, structured text conversion, text classification, database integration, data retention and security, and business policy management. He has collaborated with several corporations, including Oxford University Press, Open Text, and IBM, and served as a member of the Scientific Advisory Committee for the Business Intelligence Strategic Network (BIN). In 2005, the University of Waterloo and the City of Waterloo announced the naming of the road *Frank Tompa Drive* in recognition of Professor Tompa being one of those who "epitomize the energy and enterprise that characterize the University of Waterloo." He was named a Fellow of the ACM in 2010 and awarded a Queen Elizabeth II Diamond Jubilee Medal in 2012, both for contributions in the area of text-dominated data management.

ERIC YU

Eric Yu is Professor at the Faculty of Information, University of Toronto, Canada. His research interests are in the areas of information systems modeling and design, requirements engineering, knowledge management, and software engineering. Books he has co-authored or co-edited include: *Social Modeling for Requirements Engineering* (MIT Press, 2011); *Conceptual Modeling: Foundations and Applications* (Springer, 2009); and *Non-Functional Requirements in Software Engineering* (Springer, 2000). He is an associate editor for the *Int. Journal of Information Systems Modeling and Design*, and serves on the editorial boards of the *Int. J. of Agent Oriented Software Engineering*, *IET Software*, and the *Journal of Data Semantics*. He received his Ph.D. in Computer Science from the University of Toronto.

Printed in the United States
by Baker & Taylor Publisher Services